IMAGES
of America

REMEMBERING MICHIGAN'S CIVIL WAR SOLDIERS

6TH MICHIGAN CAVALRY TROOPERS. Sgt. Luther Kanouse (standing, left) and Sgt. Henry Coles (standing, right) enlisted in Company D, 6th Michigan Cavalry. Sergeant Kanouse was wounded at the Battle of Trevilian Station and Winchester, Virginia. Commissioned a lieutenant, after the war he resided in Byron, Michigan. Sergeant Coles, from Burns Township, Michigan, served throughout the war and was mustered out at Fort Leavenworth, Kansas, in November 1865. Coles is buried at St. George's Lutheran Cemetery in Brighton, Michigan. The other cavalrymen are unidentified. (Courtesy of Morrie Coles.)

ON THE COVER: **ORLANDO BOLIVAR WILLCOX (1823–1907).** Born in Detroit, Willcox (sitting) graduated from West Point, served in the Mexican-American War, and practiced law in his hometown. In 1861, he was a colonel with the 1st Michigan Infantry. Wounded at the First Battle of Bull Run, Willcox was captured by Confederates. Commissioned brigadier general, he commanded a division in the IX Corps, Army of the Potomac. Brevetted major general, Willcox also received the Medal of Honor. This photograph, taken in June 1864 at Cold Harbor, Virginia, shows Willcox with the 3rd Division's flag. (Courtesy of the Library of Congress.)

IMAGES
of America
REMEMBERING MICHIGAN'S CIVIL WAR SOLDIERS

David D. Finney Jr. and Judith Stermer McIntosh

ARCADIA
PUBLISHING

Copyright © 2015 by David D. Finney Jr. and Judith Stermer McIntosh
ISBN 978-1-4671-1345-8

Published by Arcadia Publishing
Charleston, South Carolina

Printed in the United States of America

Library of Congress Control Number: 2014947073

For all general information, please contact Arcadia Publishing:
Telephone 843-853-2070
Fax 843-853-0044
E-mail sales@arcadiapublishing.com
For customer service and orders:
Toll-Free 1-888-313-2665

Visit us on the Internet at www.arcadiapublishing.com

David: To my parents for instilling an appreciation of America's history, David Dorsey Finney (1919–1990) and Dorothy Elizabeth Druding Finney (1918–1979).

Judith: To history teacher Phyllis Agosti and my grandchildren, Damian, Cassondra, and Antoinette.

CONTENTS

ACKNOWLEDGMENTS

Over the years, we have benefited from the willingness of friends, collectors, and historians to share their knowledge of Michigan's Civil War history. Many have graciously shared their research and made available images from personal collections to assist in making this Arcadia Publishing volume. We are indebted to Dale R. Niesen, who enthusiastically went out of his way to offer and provide assistance in the selection of numerous images for this book. He also opened the door to several collectors who were generous in providing photographs for this publication. Similarly, we have great appreciation for the following collectors and friends who contributed to *Remembering Michigan's Civil War Soldiers:* the Armstrong family, John Beckendorf, David Broene, Robert M. Coch, Morrie Coles, Glen Fincham, John Gelderloos, Michael Hogle, Richard and Mary Hutchins, David Ingall, Cheryl Rogers, Richard Tanner, and George Wilkinson. For several of these individuals, their passion as collectors and custodians of Michigan's history is a result of the mentorship of Karl Rommel, Ray Russell, and Roger Heiple. They are all collectors of the highest caliber and stewards of Michigan's Civil War photography. This book could not have been compiled and written without their contributions.

Several institutions provided images for this book, including the Library of Congress (LOC), archivist Steven Bye at the US Army History and Education Center (USAHEC), longtime friend and historian John Heiser at Gettysburg National Military Park (GNMP), Archives of Michigan, Milford historian Linda Dagenhardt, Dr. Louis Yock at the Benzonia Museum, Joyce Fisher at the Howell Area Archives, Marilyn Gray and Elaine Smith at the Luther Area Museum, and Thomas Gerhardt, assistant director at the Manistee Museum. David is especially grateful to his daughter, Nancy A. Finney, and sister, Deborah Finney Smith, who contributed their considerable editorial skills to reviewing and improving written drafts for this publication.

Unless otherwise noted, images in *Remembering Michigan's Civil War Soldiers* are from the authors' collection.

INTRODUCTION

The sesquicentennial of the Civil War provided the motivation and opportunity to write *Remembering Michigan's Civil War Soldiers*. This publication takes us back to the war years of 1861–1865 and examines a selection of soldiers' images that serve to remind us of Michigan's patriots and heroes of that fratricidal conflict, which had unparalleled historic significance for our nation and state. More than 90,000 Wolverines participated in the Civil War, and almost 15,000 died as a result of battle wounds or diseases. This book presents unique portraits and images that attempt to convey and illustrate the personalities of Michigan's participants in the brutal and bloody battles of the American Civil War.

Michigan soldiers served as leaders and common soldiers. These men visited photographic galleries in cities and villages to have their likeness or photograph taken for family, sweethearts, friends, and comrades. Itinerant photographers followed the troops to their camps, where they erected studios in cabins and tents and advertised sample images at the tent flaps. Millions of photographs were taken during the Civil War. Some were ambrotypes on glass, or tintypes, and albumenized prints. The most popular and affordable were known as carte de visites, or visiting cards, which were about the size of modern billfold photographs. Photographers and their cameras preserved for posterity these images of Michigan soldiers, and they reveal not only their faces but also their unique and distinctive uniforms, brass insignias and badges, headgear, equipment, and weapons.

The quantity and quality of Michigan Civil War photographs available for this publication were overwhelming. More than 1,000 photographs were examined for the volume, and it was difficult to make final selections. Photographic images that had not previously been published and were of good quality were given a high priority for inclusion. The authors anticipate that this publication will be considered a useful tool or source book to help identify soldiers who were previously unidentified and provide visual information regarding uniforms, weapons, and camp equipment. These images also affirm that nothing holds our attention more than a unique and interesting photograph.

After the Confederate bombardment of Fort Sumter in Charleston, South Carolina, Michigan men joined state regiments and rapidly filled their ranks. They received brief military training at recruitment camps that were established throughout the state and were soon sent south to the theaters of rebellion. Some of the soldiers pictured in this volume rallied to the flag in 1861 and participated in the war from beginning to end. Other men, determined to exhibit their patriotic loyalty, decided to join regiments later in the war. Many Michigan military units were highly distinguished: Custer's famous Michigan Cavalry Brigade (1st, 5th, 6th, and 7th Cavalry Regiments); the 7th Michigan Infantry, known as "The Forlorn Hope of Fredericksburg;" the 24th Michigan Infantry of the Iron Brigade; Robert H.G. Minty's 4th Michigan Cavalry that captured Confederate president Jefferson Davis at Irwinville, Georgia; the 17th Michigan Infantry Regiment, known as the "Stonewall Regiment" from their baptism of fire at South Mountain,

Maryland; the Loomis Battery A, 1st Michigan Light Artillery; and the 1st Michigan Engineers and Mechanics that received accolades from Gen. William T. Sherman. From 1861 to 1865, Michiganders possessed great resolve and determination to see that the Union would not be divided and the United States torn apart.

Images of Michigan generals, officers of the line, noncommissioned officers, privates, and old veterans are included in this volume. While some Michigan generals' images were chosen for this publication, others who were well known and possessed strong Michigan connections are recognized by name, including Byron Mac Cutcheon, Gustavus Adolphus De Russy, Henry Jackson Hunt, Justus McKinstry, Robert Horatio George Minty, Henry Rutgers Mizner, Benjamin Franklin Partridge, Benjamin Dudley Pritchard, and William Alexander Throop.

There are selected images of Wolverines who were killed in battle, died of their wounds, were victims of diseases, or perished in Confederate prison camps such as Andersonville. None of those who paid the ultimate sacrifice anticipated their deaths on battlefields or in hospital wards. Likewise, they did not expect to leave behind grieving mothers, fathers, sweethearts, wives, or children. Images of soldiers who were amongst the initial recipients of the Medal of Honor are pictured in this volume. A selection of camp scenes, military bands, field musicians, and drummer boys are included. A majority of photographs examined for this volume were of unidentified Michigan soldiers; some of those images were fascinating and impressive, but a decision was made to publish photographs of identified men who served in the various branches of the Army.

The final chapter of this book allows the reader an opportunity to view a selection of Civil War veterans' photographs. The old soldiers, who annually gathered for local and state encampments and regimental reunions, relished the opportunity to renew old friendships and reminisce about the days when they fought to preserve the Union. Veterans often belonged to organizations like the Grand Army of the Republic (GAR) or the Military Order of the Loyal Legion (MOLLUS), groups that were precursors to the American Legion and Veterans of Foreign Wars.

June 12, 1889, was designated as Michigan Day at Gettysburg, and nine Michigan monuments (funding was provided by the State of Michigan) were unveiled and dedicated to honor Michigan soldiers who fought on that hallowed ground. In subsequent years, Michigan's legislature provided additional funding to place monuments at the following battlefields: Vicksburg, Shiloh, Chickamauga, and Andersonville Prison Camp. Michigan's Civil War governor, Austin Blair, was honored with a statue that is situated on the capitol grounds. Pres. William Howard Taft participated in the impressive dedication of the equestrian monument to Gen. George A. Custer that was dedicated on June 10, 1910, in Monroe, Michigan. Several magnificent monuments were erected by wealthy philanthropists in Muskegon and Jackson. Throughout Michigan's cities and counties, monuments were dedicated to the memories of the "Boys in Blue" who sacrificed so much to attain victory and preserve their beloved Union. These wonderful monuments represent our ties to the past and our appreciation and understanding of our own history.

One

WITH STARS ON

THEIR SHOULDERS

When Michiganders received the news of the Confederate attack and the subsequent surrender of Fort Sumter in Charleston, South Carolina, on April 12, 1861, it was as though a lightning bolt followed by a rolling thunderclap swept across the Great Lakes State. Patriotic fervor rapidly spread from larger cities to tiny hamlets and farming communities throughout Michigan. Public rallies were held to encourage young men to defend the Union and join the infantry, cavalry, or artillery.

Pres. Abraham Lincoln requested that Michigan supply troops to serve during the national crisis. Michigan governor Austin Blair began an immediate search to identify men possessing strong leadership qualities and military expertise to command the state's regiments. Blair recognized the importance of selecting influential political, business, agricultural, and educational leaders, and many men were commissioned to high ranks in state military organizations.

In Michigan, as in other states, professional military officers were at a premium, as were those who possessed prior military experience. Michigan generals came from all walks of life and included professional soldiers, politicians, lawyers, engineers, businessmen, manufacturers, merchants, educators, farmers, and lumbermen. During the four years of war, at least 58 Michigan men achieved the rank of brevet general. Brevet promotions were given for valor, honor, meritorious and faithful service, and distinguished conduct. The majority of the men pictured here received brevet commissions towards the end of the war, when the country could show its gratitude for faithful and distinguished service. Michigan's generals provided leadership that contributed to the preservation of the Union, and in the postwar era some of them used their military influence as a ticket to success in business or politics. The burial sites of at least 69 Civil War generals are located in communities throughout Michigan, and 17 of them rest in Detroit's Elmwood Cemetery.

IRA COREY ABBOTT (1824–1908). Abbott entered service from Burr Oak as a captain with the 1st Michigan Infantry. He was promoted to colonel in March 1863. He was wounded at the Battles of Fredericksburg and Gettysburg. Following the war, Abbott was a merchant and a clerk for the US Pension Bureau, and he is buried at Arlington National Cemetery. (Courtesy of the USAHEC.)

GEORGE SIGOURNEY ACKER (1835–1879). Born on Christmas Day in 1835, Acker joined the 1st Michigan Cavalry and became a major in 1861. He transferred to the 9th Michigan Cavalry in May 1863 and was wounded at Bean's Station, Tennessee, in November of that year. In the spring of 1864, he was promoted to colonel of the regiment. Living in Kalamazoo after the war, he operated a hotel and was a milkman. Acker is buried in Riverside Cemetery in Union City, Michigan.

RUSSELL ALEXANDER ALGER (1836–1907). A Grand Rapids lumberman, Alger was wounded and captured while serving with the 2nd Michigan Cavalry. He became lieutenant colonel of the 6th Michigan Cavalry and then colonel of the 5th Michigan Cavalry; he was wounded during the Gettysburg Campaign at Boonesboro, Maryland. Alger resigned from active service in September 1864. Brevetted major general, Alger, who was a Republican, was elected Michigan's governor, then US senator, and was later appointed secretary of war by President McKinley. He is buried in Detroit's Elmwood Cemetery. (Courtesy of Dale Niesen.)

HENRY BAXTER (1821–1873). A resident of Jonesville, Baxter joined the 7th Michigan Infantry as a captain with Company C. He was wounded in the abdomen during the Peninsular Campaign and in his left shoulder at Fredericksburg. Promoted to brigadier general in March 1863, Baxter commanded a brigade at Gettysburg. He was wounded again at the Battle of the Wilderness. President Grant appointed Baxter as minister to the Republic of Honduras. He died from pneumonia in 1873 and is buried in Jonesville's cemetery. (Courtesy of the LOC.)

HENRY BOYNTON CLITZ (1824–1888).
Born into a military family, Clitz served as a page in the Michigan Territorial Senate and graduated from West Point in 1845. Clitz served as a captain with the 3rd US Infantry, a major with the 12th US Infantry, and lieutenant colonel with the 6th US Infantry. Brevetted brigadier general on March 13, 1865, Clitz retired from the Army in 1885, and he is believed to have drowned at Niagara Falls in October 1888. His cenotaph was placed at Elmwood Cemetery in Detroit. (Courtesy of the LOC.)

JOSEPH TARR COPELAND (1813–1893).
A Mexican-American War veteran and justice of the Michigan Supreme Court, Copeland served in the 1st Michigan Cavalry and was appointed colonel with the 5th Cavalry. Commissioned a brigadier general, he commanded the Michigan Cavalry Brigade. At the Battle of Gettysburg, his brigade was given to General Custer. Assigned to a recruitment depot near Pittsburgh, Pennsylvania, he then became commandant of the prison camp at Alton, Illinois. After the war, Copeland lived at Orchard Lake, Michigan, and relocated to Orange Park, Florida, where he died. He is buried in Pontiac's Oak Hill Cemetery. (Courtesy of the USAHEC.)

GEORGE ARMSTRONG CUSTER (1839–1876).
In 1857, Custer was living with his sister in
Monroe when he received an appointment
to West Point. After graduating in 1861,
he performed staff duties for Gen. George
McClellan and Gen. Alfred Pleasonton.
At age 24, he was promoted to brigadier
general and received command of the
Michigan Cavalry Brigade. Fighting with
great distinction, in 1864 he was brevetted
major general. This photograph was
taken at Mathew Brady's Washington,
DC, studio in May 1865. After the war,
Custer commanded the 7th US Cavalry,
which he led to the Little Big Horn in
June 1876. His remains were interred at
West Point. (Courtesy of the LOC.)

CHARLES CAMP DOOLITTLE
(1832–1903). A resident of
Hillsdale, Doolittle served as
an officer in the 4th Michigan
Infantry. Appointed colonel of
the 18th Michigan Infantry in
1862, he served as provost guard at
Nashville, Tennessee. At the battle
of Nashville, he commanded the 1st
Brigade, 3rd Division, XXIII Corps.
Brevetted major general at the end
of the war, Doolittle lived in Toledo,
Ohio, worked as a banker, and
served as an elder of Westminster
Presbyterian Church. He is buried
in Toledo's Woodlawn Cemetery.

13

JAIRUS WILLIAM HALL (1840–UNKNOWN). A resident of Washtenaw County, in June 1861 Hall entered the military as a lieutenant in Company D, 4th Michigan Infantry, at Adrian. Hall was recognized for his leadership abilities and received promotions to become colonel of the regiment in July 1864. He was made a brevet brigadier general on March 13, 1865, for gallant and meritorious services. (Courtesy of George Wilkinson.)

GEORGE LUCAS HARTSUFF (1830–1874). A resident of Livingston County and an 1852 graduate of West Point, Hartsuff was wounded twice in the Third Seminole War. He served as chief of staff to General Rosecrans and was with General McDowell's corps during the Second Battle of Bull Run. At Antietam, he received a serious wound, which disabled him for months. Hartsuff returned to duty in March 1865 and was given command of forces between the James and Appomattox Rivers. He retired as a major general in 1871 and died three years later. He is buried at West Point. (Courtesy of the USAHEC.)

WILLIAM POWER INNES (1826–1893). Prior to the war, Innes was a distinguished civil engineer engaged in railroad construction. He organized the 1st Michigan Engineers and Mechanics. This regiment was commended for constructing forts, bridges, field works, repairing roads, and fighting as infantry when necessary. Brevetted brigadier general on March 13, 1865, after the war Innes continued a career as a civil engineer and insurance agent. He is buried in the Fulton Street Cemetery in Grand Rapids. (Courtesy of Michael Hogle.)

HEBER LEFAVOUR (1837–1878). In Detroit at the outbreak of war, LeFavour was commissioned captain of Company F, 5th Michigan Infantry. He was wounded on the left side of his face at Williamsburg, Virginia, on May 5, 1862. Appointed colonel of the 22nd Michigan Infantry, he was taken prisoner at the Battle of Chickamauga, Georgia, on September 20, 1863. He was brevetted brigadier general and mustered out at Nashville, Tennessee, on June 26, 1865. Following the war, LeFavour was a merchant and manufacturer and served as the adjutant general of Rhode Island. He died in February 1878 and is buried at Swan Point Cemetery in Providence, Rhode Island.

ALLYNE CUSHING LITCHFIELD (1835–1911). A Massachusetts businessman working in Michigan's lumber industry when the war began, Litchfield joined the 5th Michigan Cavalry as a captain with Company B. Commissioned lieutenant colonel with the 7th Michigan Cavalry in November 1862, Litchfield was captured on March 1, 1864, during Gen. Judson Kilpatrick's raid on Richmond, Virginia. Litchfield became colonel of the 7th Cavalry and received a brevet brigadier general's commission on March 13, 1865. He is buried in Marshfield Hills Cemetery in Marshfield, Massachusetts. (Courtesy of the USAHEC.)

DWIGHT MAY (1822–1880). An 1849 graduate of the University of Michigan, May practiced law at Battle Creek before moving to Kalamazoo. In 1861, he was captain with Company I, 2nd Michigan Infantry, and was later promoted to colonel with the 12th Michigan Infantry. This regiment served in western Tennessee, Mississippi, and Arkansas. He received a brevet brigadier general's commission in October 1865. May became Michigan's lieutenant governor and attorney general. He died in 1880 and is buried at Mountain Home Cemetery in Kalamazoo. (Courtesy of Dale Niesen.)

JOHN KEMP MIZNER (1834–1898).
Mizner graduated from the US Military
Academy at West Point in 1856. He was
a captain with the 2nd US Cavalry and
colonel of the 3rd Michigan Cavalry.
He was brevetted brigadier general in
March 1865 for gallant and meritorious
service. His brother Henry R. Mizner
was also a general officer. Mizner was
a career Army officer, retiring as a
brigadier general in 1897, and he is buried
at Arlington National Cemetery.

HENRY ANDREW MORROW (1829–1891).
Morrow was serving as judge of Detroit's
recorder's court when he raised the 24th
Michigan Infantry. Colonel Morrow was
wounded at Gettysburg, the Battle of
the Wilderness, and Petersburg, Virginia.
He was brevetted major general and
became a career Army officer. Morrow
was a Master Mason and is buried in
Niles's Silver Brook Cemetery.

JOHN MORRISON OLIVER (1828–1872). In Monroe, Oliver was a pharmacist and court recorder. An officer in the 4th Michigan Infantry, he was appointed colonel of the 15th Michigan Infantry, which he led at Shiloh, Tennessee. The 15th fought at Vicksburg, Mississippi, and during the Atlanta Campaign. Oliver commanded a brigade on Sherman's March to the Sea and through the Carolinas. Brevetted major general at the end of the war, Oliver practiced law in Little Rock, Arkansas, and died in Washington, DC. He is buried in Lake View Cemetery in Penn Yan, New York. (Courtesy of Dale Niesen.)

JOHN GIBSON PARKHURST (1824–1906). An attorney in Coldwater, Parkhurst became a lieutenant colonel with the 9th Michigan Infantry. Captured at the First Battle of Murfreesboro in July 1862, he was later appointed provost marshal with the XIV Corps and was brevetted brigadier general. Pres. Andrew Johnson appointed him a US marshal for Michigan. He was a member of the GAR, National Union Veterans' Association, Democratic Party, and Episcopal Church. He is buried at Oak Grove Cemetery in Coldwater. (Courtesy of Michael Hogle.)

BYRON ROOT PIERCE (1829–1924). A Grand Rapids dentist, Pierce became a colonel with the 3rd Michigan Infantry. Wounded five times during the war, the Gettysburg injury to his left leg would require eventual amputation. He commanded a brigade and division during General Grant's Overland Campaign and received a brevet promotion to major general. Pierce was a member of the GAR and MOLLUS and was Michigan's last living Civil War general. He is buried at Fulton Street Cemetery in Grand Rapids.

ORLANDO METCALFE POE (1832–1895). A West Point graduate and colonel with the 2nd Michigan Infantry, Poe commanded a brigade at the Second Battle of Bull Run and Fredericksburg, Virginia. He was chief engineer of the XXIII Corps and for the Army of the Ohio. Poe provided engineering service during General Sherman's Georgia and Carolina campaigns and was brevetted brigadier general. He is buried in Arlington National Cemetery. (Courtesy of the LOC.)

CHARLES EDWARD SMITH (1824–1907).
A farmer and resident of Oshtemo, Smith joined the 11th Michigan Cavalry as a major in August 1863, and he rose to command the regiment. Smith received brevets to colonel and brigadier general. In the postwar years, he was a lawyer and real estate agent. Smith is buried at Mountain Home Cemetery in Kalamazoo. (Courtesy of Richard Tanner.)

GEORGE SPALDING (1836–1915). A teacher prior to the war, in June 1861 Spalding joined the 4th Michigan Infantry. Rising through the ranks, he became captain of Company B and was wounded in the neck at Malvern Hill during the Seven Days Campaign in Virginia. Recovering from the wound, he was promoted to lieutenant colonel. Spalding was appointed colonel of the 12th Tennessee Cavalry (US) and promoted brevet brigadier general. Spalding was a lawyer, banker, congressman, and member of the GAR, Presbyterian Church, and Masonic Fraternity. He is buried in Monroe's Woodland Cemetery. (Courtesy of Robert Coch.)

HENRY DWIGHT TERRY (1812–1869).
A Detroit lawyer, Terry organized
the 5th Michigan Infantry, which he
commanded at Williamsburg and Seven
Pines, Virginia. Promoted to brigadier
general, Terry commanded a brigade in
Corcoran's division at Suffolk, Virginia,
and a division of the VI Corps in the fall
of 1863. He commanded Johnson's Island
Prison, resigning in February 1865. He
practiced law in Washington, DC, and
is buried in Clinton Grove Cemetery in
Mount Clemens. (Courtesy of the LOC.)

LUTHER S. TROWBRIDGE (1836–1912).
Trowbridge was born and raised in Oakland
County, attended Yale University for a
time, and eventually settled in Detroit. He
served in the 5th Michigan Cavalry as a
major. In 1863, he was assigned to the 10th
Michigan Cavalry as lieutenant colonel
and received a brevet major general's
commission in June 1865. Trowbridge
was a lawyer, US Internal Revenue
collector, Republican, and member of
Detroit's GAR Post No. 384 and both the
Congregational and Presbyterian Churches.
His burial site is in Detroit's Elmwood
Cemetery. (Courtesy of the LOC.)

CHARLES WAITE (1837–1898). A Rockland schoolteacher, he was lieutenant in the 27th Michigan Infantry. This IX Corps regiment saw action at Vicksburg, Mississippi, and was with General Grant during the 1864 Overland Campaign. Wounded at Spotsylvania, Virginia, Waite was promoted regimental colonel. He was brevetted brigadier general in April 1864 for conspicuous gallantry in the assault on Petersburg, Virginia. After the war, he was a merchant and banker in Stephenson County, Illinois. (Courtesy of Michael Hogle.)

ALPHEUS STARKEY WILLIAMS (1810–1878). A graduate of Yale, Williams practiced law in Detroit. He was a probate judge, newspaper owner, veteran of the Mexican-American War, and postmaster of Detroit. He fought at Antietam, Chancellorsville, and Gettysburg and commanded a division in the XX Corps. He was politically active in Michigan's Democratic Party and died of a stroke in Washington, DC, during his second term in Congress. He is interred at Elmwood Cemetery in Detroit. (Courtesy of the LOC.)

Two

OFFICERS AND GENTLEMEN OF REGIMENTS AND COMPANIES

The officers' images in this chapter represent men who were commissioned as lieutenants, captains, majors, lieutenant colonels, and colonels. The phrase "Duty, Honor, and Country" is applicable to these officers that commanded Michigan's regiments and batteries during the war. Their responsibilities were similar to those of modern officers serving in America's military. They were selected as leaders because of their loyalty, devotion to the country, and willingness to exhibit personal courage in battle situations. Responsibilities included administrative duties, enforcement of their commander's orders, training soldiers to prepare for battle, delegating responsibilities to subordinates, and recognizing leadership skills and attributes.

The officers were responsible for their men being fed, clothed, and remaining healthy when in the field and campaigning. It was necessary that soldiers in companies and regiments had proper equipment, particularly weapons and ammunition when on the verge of battles. Officers had to ensure that soldiers had adequate inventories of everything needed, from muskets and ammunition to food, clothing, tents, horses, and transportation.

As officers were promoted and ascended in rank, they were expected to assume additional responsibilities and expand and improve their leadership skills. Those officers who were able to create confidence and trust in their men generally commanded companies and regiments that were loyal and respected their commanders. Men in the ranks willingly followed their officers' orders when they admired and trusted their leaders.

In the years and decades following the war, many of these officers contributed to Michigan's development and were also involved in westward expansion. In postwar decades, some officers migrated to Arizona, California, Colorado, Idaho, and even Alaska. Another officer established the Texas League's Galveston baseball team. Others were successful in political, educational, religious, and business pursuits. One colonel was instrumental in helping establish Pewabic Pottery and designed the interiors of the Pullman Palace railroad cars. They also carried the emotional, physical, and mental scars of war throughout the remainder of their lives. Reflected in the images and captions of this chapter are Michigan officers who were devoted and committed to saving their country.

21ST MICHIGAN INFANTRY OFFICERS. In the spring of 1863, Col. William B. McCreery and 22 other officers of the battle-hardened 21st Michigan Infantry posed for this outdoor portrait somewhere in the hills of southern Tennessee. The bearded McCreery is seated and wearing a double-breasted frock coat. At the colonel's left are two officers playing chess. Most of the officers are equipped with Model 1860 Light Cavalry officer's swords. (Courtesy of the LOC.)

MICHIGAN CAVALRY BRIGADE OFFICERS. This albumen image, taken prior to June 13, 1863, contains the following officers from left to right: (first row) unidentified and Smith Hastings (5th Cavalry); (second row) unidentified, Col. Ebenezer Gould (5th Cavalry), Col. Russell Alger (6th Cavalry), and unidentified; (third row) unidentified, Walter Stevenson (5th Cavalry), unidentified, Peter Weber (6th Cavalry), William B. Williams (5th Cavalry), and Charles E. Bolza (6th Cavalry).

GEORGE A. ARMSTRONG. From Eaton Rapids, Armstrong was captain of Company D, 7th Michigan Cavalry. He was promoted assistant quartermaster and served on the staff of Gen. Judson Kilpatrick. Armstrong stood with Kilpatrick in several photographs taken at Stevensburg, Virginia, in 1864. (Courtesy of Michael Hogle.)

WILLIAM A. ATWOOD. Living in Ypsilanti, Atwood became captain of Company E, 1st Michigan Cavalry. Promoted to major, he was captured during the Second Battle of Bull Run on August 30, 1862, and sent to Libby Prison. After his release from Confederate prison, he completed his service as a captain with the 30th Michigan Infantry.

25

BENJAMIN F. AXTELL AND ROBERT F. JUDSON. Leaving his wife and two daughters in Kalamazoo, Captain Axtell (left) joined the 5th Michigan Cavalry in September 1862. He was mortally wounded at Yellow Tavern, Virginia, on May 11, 1864, and died at Libby Prison. In this carte de visite image, Axtell sits with his friend Capt. Robert Judson, who was acting assistant inspector general at Michigan Cavalry Brigade headquarters. (Courtesy of John Beckendorf.)

BENJAMIN F. BAILEY. A resident of Holland, Michigan, Bailey enlisted in Company D, 2nd Michigan Cavalry, as a sergeant. Captured by Confederates at Blountsville, Kentucky, on December 31, 1862, he was released six months later. Bailey was commissioned a lieutenant on New Year's Day 1863 and served until March 1864. In this image, Bailey's Hardee hat emblazoned with crossed sabers rests on his knee, and he is clutching his gauntlets. (Courtesy of David Broene.)

EDWARD BATEWELL. This carte de visite of Doctor Batewell shows a dangling square and compass watch fob, indicating his Masonic affiliation. Batewell served as surgeon for the 14th Michigan Infantry and acting brigade surgeon in 1863. He was brevetted lieutenant colonel, US Volunteers, in June 1865. He is buried in Ypsilanti's Highland Cemetery. (Courtesy of David Broene.)

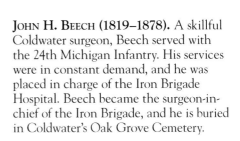

JOHN H. BEECH (1819–1878). A skillful Coldwater surgeon, Beech served with the 24th Michigan Infantry. His services were in constant demand, and he was placed in charge of the Iron Brigade Hospital. Beech became the surgeon-in-chief of the Iron Brigade, and he is buried in Coldwater's Oak Grove Cemetery.

Hudson B. Blackman. This quarter-plate ambrotype depicts Blackman as an officer in the 5th Michigan Infantry. He served as regimental quartermaster and was promoted to brevet major at the end of the war. He was a partner in the Howell Foundry and a member of the Presbyterian Church. Blackman died in 1896 and is buried at Lakeview Cemetery in Howell. (Courtesy of the Howell Area Archives.)

Simon Brennan. In this image, Captain Brennan, of the 3rd Michigan Infantry, wears a bearskin hat. From Ottawa County, Brennan suffered wounds in the left arm at Fair Oaks and right shoulder at Groveton, Virginia. Wounded again at the Battle of the Wilderness, he was taken prisoner. Brennan was in POW camps at Macon, Georgia, and Charleston and Columbia, South Carolina. Two of his brothers were killed in the war. After the war, he was a farmer, Republican, and member of the GAR in Manton, Michigan. (Courtesy of David Broene.)

NATHAN CHURCH (1840–1926). Enlisting as sergeant with the 8th Michigan Infantry in August 1861, Church was discharged for disability six months later. He reentered service in the 26th Michigan Infantry and was promoted from adjutant to lieutenant colonel. Gen. Nelson Miles requested Church as his assistant adjutant general at the end of the war. Church became one of the jailers for Confederate president Jefferson Davis. After the war, he was a successful merchant, banker, and farmer and was quartermaster general for Michigan's state militia. Church is buried in the Ithaca Cemetery. (Courtesy of Dale Niesen.)

RICHARD S. DILLON (c. 1830–1886). In the Detroit iron business, Dillon was presented a sword from the Molder's Association at the organization of the 24th Michigan Infantry. He attained the rank of major and was wounded four times on July 1, 1863, at Gettysburg. Dillon was appointed the acting assistant inspector general of the Iron Brigade and served with the regiment throughout the war. After the war, Dillon was a member of the Detroit Fairbanks Post No. 17 of the GAR.

HORACE W. DODGE. Residing in Detroit, Dodge joined Company C, 5th Michigan Cavalry, as a lieutenant. Commissioned a captain in April 1863, he was wounded in the left hip on June 12, 1864, at the Battle of Trevilian Station and discharged on account of the wounds. Dodge was brevetted major for gallant and meritorious services. This image was taken at Stevensburg, Virginia, during the winter encampment of the Michigan Cavalry Brigade. (Courtesy of John Beckendorf.)

CHARLES DUPONT. Look closely at Dupont's profile and note the patch that covers his right eye. Dupont, who was from Adrian, was seriously wounded at the Battle of Gaines's Mill on June 27, 1862, and was discharged for disability from Company K, 4th Michigan Infantry. He became captain of the 13th Battery, Michigan Light Artillery, and assisted in the defense of Washington, DC, in July 1864, when Confederate forces attacked Fort Stevens. Dupont was a member of Detroit's GAR Post No. 384. (Courtesy of the USAHEC.)

ELI F. EVANS. A confident-looking lieutenant, Evans is posed holding his officer's sword with his sash hanging from the waist. He enlisted in Company D, 9th Michigan Infantry, and was commissioned lieutenant of Company B, 28th Michigan Infantry. Evans was mustered out of service at Raleigh, North Carolina, on June 5, 1866. (Courtesy of David Broene.)

THADDEUS FOOTE (1821–1903). A graduate of Yale University and Harvard Law School, Foote served as major with the 6th Michigan Cavalry. Promoted to colonel with the 10th Michigan Cavalry in September 1863, Foote was discharged for disability in July 1864. He was a lawyer and US pension agent in Grand Rapids. Foote is buried at the Fulton Street Cemetery in Grand Rapids. (Courtesy of the USAHEC.)

CHARLES FOX AND COMRADE. A citizen from Pontiac, Fox (left) entered Company G, 4th Michigan Infantry, as a lieutenant in July 1864. He was commissioned captain of Company H in October 1865 and discharged at Houston, Texas, on May 26, 1866. The other officer in this quarter-plate tintype is unidentified.

JOHN G. GILBERT. Lieutenant Gilbert, from Lockport, was commissioned an officer in Company E, 25th Michigan Infantry. He earlier served as first sergeant, Company G. In this carte de visite, he is posed with an officer's saber cradled in his arm and his kepi placed on the table. (Courtesy of David Broene.)

WILLIAM GOODALE. He lived in the far north of Michigan at Houghton and enlisted in Company I, 23rd Infantry, as sergeant in July 1862. Goodale served as first sergeant, commissary sergeant, and was commissioned to captain Company F in 1865. He was mustered out at Salisbury, North Carolina, on June 28, 1865. (Courtesy of Robert Coch.)

EBENEZER GOULD (1818–1877). A practicing attorney and businessman in Owosso prior to the war, Gould joined the 5th Michigan Cavalry and became colonel of the regiment. He was wounded during the Gettysburg Campaign at Hagerstown, Maryland, on July 12, 1863. Gould continued as a lawyer after the war, but he never recovered from his wounds and poor health. He is buried in Owosso's Oak Hill Cemetery. (Courtesy of the USAHEC.)

CLAUDIUS BUCHANAN GRANT (1835–1921). A graduate of the University of Michigan and principal of Ann Arbor High School, in July 1862 Grant began recruiting for Company D, 20th Michigan Infantry. He rose through the officer's ranks and was commissioned regimental colonel in December 1864. After the war, Grant became a lawyer and chief justice of the Michigan Supreme Court. He is buried in Ann Arbor's Forest Hill Cemetery. (Courtesy of Dale Niesen.)

WILLIAM HENRY GRAVES (1836–1874). Residing in Adrian, Graves entered the service as captain, Company K, 1st Michigan Infantry. Wounded in the left leg at the First Battle of Bull Run, July 21, 1861, he was later promoted to colonel, 12th Michigan Infantry, and was a brigade commander from July 1863 to June 1865. Graves was wounded in the right knee at Gregory's Landing, Arkansas, on September 4, 1864. He is buried in Adrian's Oakwood Cemetery. (Courtesy of David Broene.)

Caleb Griffith. A resident of Lowell, Griffith enlisted in Company C, 7th Michigan Cavalry, in August 1862. He was wounded in action at Gettysburg on July 4, 1863. Griffith was commissioned a lieutenant, Company F, 102nd USCT (1st Michigan Colored Infantry), in January 1864. He resigned his commission in August 1865. (Courtesy of GNMP.)

Charles E. Grisson. In June 1861, Livingston County resident Charles Grisson enlisted in Company D, 4th Michigan Infantry, at Adrian. He was promoted to lieutenant with Company E, 26th Infantry, in September 1862. Grisson was wounded at the Battle of Spotsylvania on May 12, 1864. He was commissioned captain and adjutant and detailed as brigade inspector, receiving the brevet of major in March 1865. He died in St. Johns, Michigan, on November 20, 1882. (Courtesy of George Wilkinson.)

NORMAN JONATHAN HALL (1837–1867). In 1854, Hall left Raisinville, Michigan, for West Point. As an artillery officer, he was present at John Brown's execution and then served as adjutant for Maj. Robert Anderson at Fort Sumter. This image was taken in New York after Fort Sumter's surrender. Hall served on McClellan's staff and was promoted to colonel of the 7th Michigan Infantry. Following the Battle of Gettysburg, he was placed on the disabled list. Hall died of disease and is buried at West Point Military Academy.

SMITH HUGH HASTINGS (1843–1905). Born in Branch County, Hastings joined the 1st Michigan Infantry. Commissioned lieutenant, 5th Michigan Cavalry, Hastings was wounded in the foot and groin at the June 1864 Battle of Trevilian Station. He was the last colonel of the 5th Michigan Cavalry. After the war, he lived in Denver, Colorado, where he was a successful merchant. Hastings is buried in Denver's Riverside Cemetery.

JOSEPH CARL HERKNER (1840–1914). Trained as clerk and watch repairman, Herkner was commissioned a lieutenant in the 1st Michigan Engineers and Mechanics. He was the youngest officer in the regiment and was promoted to captain in January 1864. He opened the Herkner Jewelry Company in Grand Rapids after the war and was active with Masonic organizations, the state militia, and St. Mark's Episcopal Church. He is buried in the Fulton Street Cemetery, Grand Rapids.

BORDEN MILLS HICKS. Borden Hicks enlisted at Three Rivers and was a sergeant in Company E, 11th Michigan Infantry. He was commissioned lieutenant and captain in the regiment and was mustered out at Sturgis, Michigan, in September 1864. (Courtesy of David Broene.)

ANDREW J. HOBART. A resident of Jackson, Michigan, Hobart joined the 1st Michigan Infantry as assistant surgeon on August 17, 1861, at Ann Arbor. Commissioned regimental surgeon in December 1862, Doctor Hobart was mustered out and honorably discharged at the expiration of his term of service in Detroit on October 7, 1864. (Courtesy of the USAHEC.)

SEYMOUR HOWELL. This portrait was taken on his wedding day, April 6, 1864. Born in England, Howell settled in Washtenaw County and worked on a farm. In 1861, he joined Company F, 6th Michigan Infantry, and was commissioned a lieutenant. This regiment was one of the first to occupy New Orleans, Louisiana, and fought at Baton Rouge and the Siege of Port Hudson. In 1863, the regiment was converted into heavy artillery and was at the surrender of Fort Morgan and Mobile, Alabama. After the war, Howell was a banker in Adrian and served as a major in the Spanish-American War. (Courtesy of David Broene.)

EDWIN M. HULBURD. Living in Hudson when the war began, Hulburd joined Company A, 18th Michigan Infantry, as a captain. He was promoted to major in February 1864 and became the acting assistant inspector general, 1st Brigade, 4th Division, XX Corps, from March to July 1865. Commissioned to lieutenant colonel in March 1865, Hulburd was mustered out at Nashville, Tennessee, on June 26, 1865. (Courtesy of Michael Hogle.)

ANDREW J. ITSELL. Raised in Howell and a graduate of normal school, Itsell enlisted in the 1st Michigan Sharpshooters. He later received a captain's commission and command of Company K, 10th Michigan Cavalry. His two brothers, Stephen and Paul, served with him. After the war, Captain Itsell moved to San Francisco, California, where he married, became a professor of education, and raised two daughters. (Courtesy of the USAHEC.)

ROBERT KNAGGS. A resident of Monroe County, Knaggs enlisted in Company D, 7th Michigan Infantry, at the age of 25 in August 1861. Commissioned a lieutenant, Knaggs served as an aide-de-camp on the staff of Gen. Henry Baxter, II Corps, and was taken prisoner at Gettysburg on July 1, 1863, and released in March 1864. He completed the war serving on General Baxter's staff and was made a brevet captain for gallant and meritorious services.

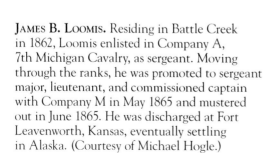

JAMES B. LOOMIS. Residing in Battle Creek in 1862, Loomis enlisted in Company A, 7th Michigan Cavalry, as sergeant. Moving through the ranks, he was promoted to sergeant major, lieutenant, and commissioned captain with Company M in May 1865 and mustered out in June 1865. He was discharged at Fort Leavenworth, Kansas, eventually settling in Alaska. (Courtesy of Michael Hogle.)

CHARLES MATTHEW LUM (1831–1899). A professional artist, Lum established a studio in Detroit. A member of the Detroit Light Guard, he was elected captain, Company A, 1st Michigan Infantry. After recovering from a wound received at the First Battle of Bull Run, Lum was appointed colonel, 10th Michigan Infantry. He commanded a brigade in the XXIV Army Corps and was mustered out in April 1865. Lum encouraged Mary Chase Perry, inspiring her to create Pewabic Pottery. Lum himself designed Pullman Palace railroad cars. He is buried at Elmwood Cemetery in Detroit.

WILLIAM D'ALTON MANN (1839–1920). Entering the military in Company E, 1st Michigan Cavalry, as a captain, Mann became lieutenant colonel with the 5th Michigan Cavalry and colonel in the 7th Michigan Cavalry. His greatest day as a commander was July 3, 1863, at Gettysburg, where he led his regiment in battle and received accolades from General Custer. A businessman in New York City, he was a member of MOLLUS and the Episcopal Church. He died from pneumonia and is buried at Woodlawn Cemetery in the Bronx. (Courtesy of the USAHEC.)

JAMES MCPHERSON. At the end of his service, Captain McPherson commanded the Provost Guard, 2nd Division, II Corps. He enlisted in Company F, 7th Michigan Infantry, as first sergeant, was commissioned lieutenant and captain, and participated in 31 battles and skirmishes with the regiment. After the war, McPherson lived in Lowell and is buried in Milford. (Courtesy of the Armstrong family.)

PETER D. MONTGOMERY. Montgomery joined the 6th Michigan Infantry at Eaton Rapids and was commissioned captain on September 1, 1862. Montgomery was wounded in action while fighting at Port Hudson, Louisiana, on May 27, 1863. This image is a beautiful, hand-colored albumen.

FREDERICK AUGUSTUS NIMS (1841–1921). A resident of Monroe, Nims enlisted in Company C, 5th Michigan Cavalry, as first sergeant in August 1862. He was commissioned lieutenant with Company F in January 1864. Appointed an aide-de-camp on Gen. George Custer's staff, Nims served from July to September 1864. Promoted to first lieutenant, Company B, in March 1865, he was honorably discharged in August 1865. After the war, he was a farmer and member of the GAR. Nims is buried next to the Custer family at Monroe's Woodland Cemetery. (Courtesy of John Beckendorf.)

JAMES S. RANSOM. From Kalamazoo, Michigan, Ransom joined Company H, 44th Illinois Infantry, as a lieutenant on July 1, 1861. He was promoted and appointed adjutant in June 1862 and captain, Company D, on March 5, 1863. He mustered out of service in September 1865. This regiment was engaged in some of the major battles in the western theater. (Courtesy of Richard Tanner.)

GEORGE H. RATHBUN. A resident of Adrian, 19-year-old Rathbun joined Company D, 4th Michigan Infantry, in August 1864. Commissioned captain and appointed an aide-de-camp on the staff of Brevet Brigadier General Wisner on January 1, 1866, Rathbun mustered out in May 1866 at Houston, Texas. (Courtesy of George Wilkinson.)

JOHN VALENTINE RUEHLE (1813–1891). Born in Germany, he was the first captain of the Detroit Scott Guards in the 1840s and served in the 1st Michigan Infantry in the Mexican-American War. A grocer and baker by trade, Ruehle was also active in Detroit politics. He was lieutenant colonel, 16th Michigan Infantry, and a member of Detroit's GAR Post No. 384.

CHAUNCEY SHEPARD. From Owosso, Shepard was commissioned lieutenant, Company B, 4th Michigan Cavalry, in August 1862. He joined the 10th Michigan Cavalry in July 1863 and was promoted to captain of Company F. In February 1864, Shepard was honorably discharged on account of disability. (Courtesy of David Broene.)

WILLIAM HENRY SINCLAIR (1839–1897). A Jonesville resident, Sinclair enlisted in the 7th Michigan Infantry and then joined Battery C, 1st Michigan Light Artillery. He was appointed aide-de-camp to Gen. David Stanley and promoted to brevet colonel in March 1865. Considered a natural staff officer with a gift for the complex regulations and paperwork requirements of the Army, he also established the Freedmen's Bureau in Galveston, Texas. Sinclair served in the Texas Legislature, was a member of the GAR, MOLLUS, and Masons, and formed the Texas League's Galveston baseball team. (Courtesy of Michael Hogle.)

WATSON B. SMITH. A Detroit resident, Smith enlisted in the 5th Michigan Cavalry. He was commissioned lieutenant and commissary officer for the 8th Michigan Cavalry. Smith was also appointed acting assistant adjutant general on Gen. William Sanders's staff and promoted to captain. He was captured during Stoneman's Raid after the Battle of Sunshine Church in Georgia. Brevetted colonel, Smith lived in Omaha, Nebraska, where he was a clerk of the US Circuit Court. Smith was murdered for his support of blue laws, which forced tavern owners to pay licensing fees and close their businesses on Sundays. (Courtesy of Michael Hogle.)

WALTER STEVENSON (C. 1841–1865). Born in England and residing in Detroit, Stevenson enlisted in Company D, 5th Michigan Cavalry, as quartermaster sergeant in August 1862. He was promoted to captain and wounded at Winchester, Virginia, on September 19, 1864. His accidental and tragic death occurred in Detroit on July 9, 1865, when his horse slipped, falling on him. Stevenson is buried at Elmwood Cemetery in Detroit.

FREDERICK S. STEWART. This carte de visite shows Adjutant Stewart with gauntlets, fancy new boots with spurs, and Old Glory draped behind his left shoulder. A Pontiac resident, Stewart enlisted in the 10th Michigan Infantry as sergeant major in November 1861. He was promoted to lieutenant and adjutant in May 1862 and honorably discharged on July 9, 1864.

THOMAS BAYLIS WHITMARSH STOCKTON (1805–1890). An 1827 West Point graduate, Stockton served with the Corps of Topographical Engineers in Michigan and the Great Lakes region. During the Mexican-American War, he was colonel of the 1st Michigan Volunteers. The California gold rush enticed Stockton to move west, where he remained for six years. In 1861, he was appointed colonel, 16th Michigan Infantry. Captured at the Battle of Gaines' Mill in Virginia, Stockton was sent to Libby Prison. He resigned his commission in 1863 and returned to Flint. A successful businessman, Stockton died in 1890 and is buried at Flint's Glenwood Cemetery.

JOSEPH ALBERT SUDBOROUGH (1843–1915). Born in Hillsdale and raised in Adrian, Sudborough joined the 1st Michigan Infantry and fought on July 21, 1861, at Bull Run. He enlisted in the 17th Michigan Infantry as first sergeant, Company A, participated in all the battles of the regiment, and was promoted to captain and adjutant. After the war, he lived in St. Louis, Missouri, and was a member of the GAR and MOLLUS. Sudborough is buried at Jefferson Barracks National Cemetery.

CHARLES H. TOWN (1827–1865). A Detroiter and colonel, 1st Michigan Cavalry, Town was wounded at the Second Battle of Bull Run. With assistance from General Custer, Town led his regiment in the famous charge on July 3, 1863, at Gettysburg, which defeated Gen. J.E.B. Stuart's Confederate cavalry. Discharged for disability from wounds and advanced stages of tuberculosis, he died on May 7, 1865, and is buried at Hudson Cemetery in Hudson Mills, Michigan.

MICHAEL JAMES VREELAND (1838–1876).
Vreeland was brevetted brigadier general
on March 13, 1865, for gallant and
meritorious service. In June 1861, the
Brownstown native enlisted in Company
I, 4th Michigan Infantry, as sergeant, and
he rose through the ranks. Lieutenant
Vreeland was seriously wounded when a
bullet struck him through the back and
tore through his lungs at Gettysburg
on July 2, 1863. At the end of his
service, he was a lieutenant colonel
and was discharged in Houston, Texas,
in May 1866. He became a lighthouse
keeper and died at age 38 from his
Gettysburg wound. Vreeland is buried
at Woodmere Cemetery in Detroit.
(Courtesy of George Wilkinson.)

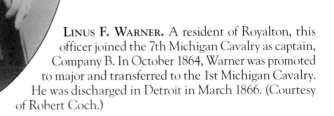

LINUS F. WARNER. A resident of Royalton, this
officer joined the 7th Michigan Cavalry as captain,
Company B. In October 1864, Warner was promoted
to major and transferred to the 1st Michigan Cavalry.
He was discharged in Detroit in March 1866. (Courtesy
of Robert Coch.)

AMASA BROWN WATSON (1826–1888). A major in the 8th Michigan Infantry, Watson was shot through the thigh on January 1, 1862, at Port Royal, South Carolina. At the Battle of Secessionville, his horse was shot from under him. He was discharged for disability in September 1862. Watson made a fortune in the lumber business in Grand Rapids, and he was active in Republican politics and MOLLUS. He is buried in Oak Hill Cemetery in Grand Rapids.

JOHN S. WATTS. An Adrian physician, Watts joined the 4th Michigan Infantry late in the summer of 1862. Watts became the regiment's assistant surgeon. He served with the 4th Regiment until honorably discharged in Detroit on June 28, 1864. (Courtesy of the USAHEC.)

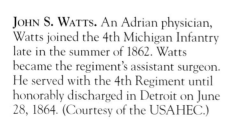

WILLIAM C. WAY (1824–1896). A Methodist minister from Plymouth, Way served with the 24th Michigan Infantry. Reverend Way was the only chaplain of a Michigan regiment who remained in service for the duration of the war. He was also the field correspondent for the *Detroit Tribune*. After the war, Reverend Way was active in the GAR and the Masonic Fraternity. He is buried in Leslie, Michigan.

WILLIAM H. WHEELER. Living in Adrian at the outbreak of the war, Wheeler enlisted in Company E, 1st Michigan Cavalry, as a corporal. He was commissioned a lieutenant in November 1862 and appointed aide-de-camp on General Custer's staff in April 1863. Wheeler mustered out of the Army in October 1864. (Courtesy of Robert Coch.)

EDWIN A. WILSON. From Paw Paw in Van Buren County, Wilson enlisted as corporal, Company C, 1st US Sharpshooters, on August 21, 1861, at Detroit. Wilson was promoted to lieutenant and wounded at the Virginia Battles of Chancellorsville on May 3, 1863, and Cold Harbor on June 4, 1864. After the war, Wilson resided in Warwick, Oklahoma. (Courtesy of Michael Hogle.)

J. HAMILTON WOODMAN. This carte de visite reveals Woodman wearing epaulettes of a first lieutenant and the infantry insignia on his rakish-looking hat. Woodman, a resident of Novi, enlisted as first sergeant, Company I, 22nd Michigan Infantry, in August 1862. He was promoted to the rank of captain in December 1863 and mustered out of service at Nashville, Tennessee, in June 1865. He lived in Ypsilanti after the war. (Courtesy of Richard Tanner.)

LUCUIS C. WOODMAN. A resident of Paw Paw, Woodman was commissioned assistant surgeon, 3rd Michigan Cavalry. In October 1863, he was promoted to surgeon, 11th Michigan Cavalry. Doctor Woodman was taken prisoner at the Battle of Saltville, Virginia, on October 2, 1864, and sent to Libby Prison. He was appointed chief surgeon, 2nd Brigade, at the end of the war. Woodman died on April 11, 1883, and is buried at Paw Paw. (Courtesy of Richard Tanner.)

EDWARD V. WRIGHT. A resident of Detroit, Wright entered service as a lieutenant, Battery B, 1st Michigan Light Artillery. Commissioned lieutenant in September 1863, Wright was wounded with two other artillerymen on May 16, 1864, at Rome Cross Roads, Georgia. Wright's cannons were engaged on November 22, 1864, in the fight at Griswoldville, Georgia. He was commissioned captain on March 14, 1865, and mustered out of service on June 14, 1865. (Courtesy of David Broene.)

GEORGE WILHELMUS MANCIUS YATES (1842–1876). He enlisted in Company A, 4th Michigan Infantry, and was promoted to lieutenant. Wounded at the Battle of Fredericksburg, Yates traveled to Monroe, Michigan, to recuperate and there met George A. Custer. Yates was assigned to the staff of Gen. Alfred Pleasonton and received a brevet promotion to lieutenant colonel at the war's end. He joined the regular Army and was with Custer at the Battle of the Little Big Horn, where he was killed. Yates is buried at Fort Leavenworth National Cemetery in Kansas. (Courtesy of George Wilkinson.)

JOHN B. YATES (1833–1899) AND FRIEND. After obtaining an engineering degree, Yates (right) worked for several railroads before moving to Michigan. When war broke out, he was a surveyor and civil engineer in Albion. Yates organized Company A, 1st Michigan Engineers and Mechanics, and quickly moved through the ranks. He was appointed colonel in November 1864. Yates died in Amherstburg, Ontario, Canada, and is buried in Vale Cemetery, Schenectady, New York. (Courtesy of John Gelderloos.)

Three

THE RANK AND FILE

The country had simmered on the edge of national conflict for several decades when Lincoln's election, the Southern secessionist movement, and the bombardment of Fort Sumter ignited the Civil War. A surge of patriotism swept through Michigan, and enthusiasm for war amongst all socioeconomic groups was endemic in urban and rural areas. Men left their homes and families with noble and idealistic intentions and rallied around the Stars and Stripes.

Michigan's citizens, a variety of nationalities and backgrounds cherishing many of the same ideals and values, willingly joined regiments to fight against the Confederacy. Michiganders whose heritage was Irish, Scottish, English, German, African American, Native American, and Canadian stepped forward, enlisting as privates in the infantry, cavalry, artillery, sharpshooters, engineers, or navy. These men were farmers, factory workers, lumberjacks, merchants, laborers, fishermen, and students. They varied in age and education, but a majority of these citizen soldiers possessed an interest in political and public affairs. Their absence from home motivated them to correspond with family and friends and to document their military experiences in letters and diaries. Going to war was an exciting experience for these men, and for many it was their first time to ride a train, be in uniform, fight for their country, and have their photographs taken.

The rank and file were the common soldiers. Privates, corporals, and sergeants comprised well over nine-tenths of Michigan's volunteers. Their military lives were regulated by drum and bugle calls. They all wore the dark blue coats and light blue trousers of the US Army. Their headgear was frequently decorated with insignia designating their branch of service, and brass letters and numbers identified their company and regiment. They all endured the same hardships and perils of soldier life and were a band of brothers. In this chapter, a selection of their images is presented. These photographs reflect their innocence, sense of duty, pride, and honor. They represented the very heart and soul of the Great Lakes State. We owe them a debt of gratitude, and their names deserve to be remembered.

C. Henry Smith, Alvah O. Brooks, and Henry Arnold. The three members of the 26th Michigan Infantry pictured in this tintype are, from left to right, Smith, Brooks, and Arnold. Sergeant Smith died on May 27, 1864, from wounds received at the Battle of Spotsylvania. Drummer boy Alvah Brooks served less than a month and was discharged by orders from Michigan governor Austin Blair. Corporal Arnold was discharged in October 1863 on a surgeon's certificate of disability. (Courtesy of the Archives of Michigan.)

DEXTER C. AVERY. He enlisted in Company A, 4th Michigan Infantry, on August 5, 1864. Promoted to corporal and sergeant, Avery was mustered out at Houston, Texas, and is buried at South Side Cemetery in Pontiac, Illinois.

FRED BARKER. This carte de visite shows Barker as first sergeant, Company I, 5th Michigan Infantry. Barker, who was 19 when he enlisted, was wounded at the Battle of the Wilderness and at Petersburg, Virginia. He died on November 30, 1888. (David Broene.)

CHARLES H. BARRETT. From Lenawee County, Barrett enlisted in Company G, 4th Michigan Infantry, at Adrian in June 1861. In this carte de visite image, he wears the stripes of a first sergeant. Barrett was commissioned captain of Company C in July 1865 and was mustered out at San Antonio, Texas, in February 1866. (Courtesy of George Wilkinson.)

GEORGE L. BENNETT. The well-equipped Private Bennett is pictured here with his musket, leather cartridge box draped to the side, cap box, and bayonet attached to his waist belt. A member of Company H, 22nd Michigan Infantry, Bennett was promoted to corporal on January 1, 1865. Following the war, he resided in Durand, Michigan.

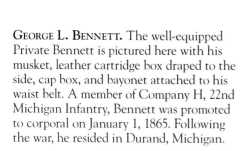

LESTER A. BERRY. A swashbuckling trooper from Croton, Private Berry's kepi device indicates he is a member of Company E, 6th Michigan Cavalry. Posing with his saber and wearing gauntlets and jackboots, Berry is ready for the field. He enlisted in the 6th Cavalry in August 1862 and mustered out in October 1865 at Fort Leavenworth, Kansas. (Courtesy of Richard Tanner.)

EZRA BROWN. A Clinton County farmer and father of six, at the age of 40 Brown enlisted in Company K, 4th Michigan Infantry, as a corporal. Promoted to sergeant, he was severely wounded on July 2, 1863, in the Wheatfield at Gettysburg. After the war, he moved to Nebraska. (Courtesy of GNMP.)

JOSEPH R. BROWN. A resident of Grand Rapids, Brown was a corporal, 3rd Michigan Infantry. He fought at the First Battle of Bull Run, through the Peninsula Campaign, the Seven Days, and the Second Battle of Bull Run, where he was wounded and left for dead on the battlefield. Brown was shot through the left thigh. Discharged on a surgeon's certificate of disability, he settled in Nunica, Michigan. (Courtesy of David Broene.)

WILLIAM A. CHILDS. Living in the far north country at Copper Harbor when war was declared, Childs enlisted as a private in Company B, 27th Michigan Infantry, in August 1862. He served as regimental commissary sergeant and was commissioned lieutenant and acting adjutant in September 1864. Brevetted captain for valor at the Battle of Fort Mahone, Virginia, on April 2, 1865, Childs marched in the Grand Review in Washington, DC. (Courtesy of Robert Coch.)

SAMUEL S. CHURCH. Proudly holding the colors of the 18th Michigan Infantry is Pvt. Samuel Church from the community of Hudson. He enlisted in Company A, 18th Michigan, for three years and was mustered out of service in June 1865 at Nashville, Tennessee. Church and the regimental colors survived the war. (Courtesy of Michael Hogle.)

STEPHEN A. COLE. Seated in a photographer's studio, Cole looks at the camera wearing his hat with an engineer's device. Cole, an artificer, was a member of Company I, 1st Michigan Engineers and Mechanics. In October 1861, he joined the regiment in Detroit and was discharged for disability at Cincinnati, Ohio, in April 1863. He lived in Grand Ledge following the war. (Courtesy of John Gelderloos.)

OLIVER M. COOK. A resident of Royal Oak, Cook enlisted at Romeo in Company B, 22nd Michigan Infantry, as a corporal in August 1862. He was promoted to sergeant in December 1864 and was mustered out of the military in June 1865. (Courtesy of Richard Tanner.)

GEORGE W. CRISLER. Posed wearing his distinctive smoking cap, Crisler, who was from Hillsdale, enlisted in Company A, 1st Sharpshooters, in December 1862 at Battle Creek. In February 1865, Private Crisler was transferred to the Veteran Reserve Corps and discharged at David's Island, New York Harbor, in September 1865. He completed his military obligation with the 4th Company, 2nd Battalion, Veteran Reserve Corps.

WILLIAM H. CRITTENDEN. This is an outstanding full plate tintype of Crittenden seated with his saber across his legs and slouch hat with devices identifying him as a member of Company E, 4th Michigan Cavalry. Corporal Crittenden was one of the troopers who captured Confederate president Jefferson F. Davis near Irwinville, Georgia, on May 10, 1865. (Courtesy of David Broene.)

JOHN C. DILLIN. Enlisting in Company K, 6th Michigan Cavalry, at Maple Grove in August 1862, Dillin was a trooper in the famous "Wolverine" Brigade that was commanded by Gen. George A. Custer. In this carte de visite image taken in Grand Rapids, Sergeant Dillin is holding his Hardee hat, which is decorated with brass devices identifying his unit. He would be discharged for disability at Washington, DC, in January 1865. (Courtesy of Michael Hogle.)

ALBERT HARRINGTON AND WILLIAM DIXON. This tintype shows two members of the 14th Michigan Infantry holding Spencer rifles. Harrington (right) and Dixon enlisted as musicians. Dixon, from Mill Point, was a drummer who was captured in January 1865 and released. Both men marched in the Grand Review in Washington, DC, on May 24, 1865, and were mustered out July 18, at Louisville, Kentucky. (Courtesy of David Broene.)

FLETCHER WILLIS HEWES (1838–1910). This carte de visite taken in Nashville, Tennessee, shows Hewes wearing the rank of ordnance sergeant. Prior to the war, he was a schoolteacher at Orion. He enlisted as a sergeant in the 10th Michigan Infantry and was commissioned to lieutenant. Hewes is the author of *History of the Formation, Movements, Camps, Scouts and Battles of the 10th Regiment Michigan Volunteer Infantry*. This history was published in 1864 and includes sketches of regimental officers. Following the war, Hewes was a school principal in Pontiac. (Courtesy of Cheryl Rogers.)

DELOSS JEWELL. Jewell was residing at Byron when he enlisted in Company A, 10th Michigan Infantry, as sergeant. Promoted to first sergeant in February 1864, and after reenlisting, Jewell was commissioned adjutant and captain, Company D. After the war, he lived in Jackson, Michigan.

ANDREW JACKSON KIMBALL (1842–1907). A resident of St. Clair County, Kimball enlisted in Company K, 2nd Michigan Cavalry, at Port Huron in September 1861. He was discharged at Nashville, Tennessee, in October 1864. In this photograph, Private Kimball wears a Hardee hat with crossed saber device and letter indicating Company K. He is wearing a shell jacket with a sword belt and a saber.

LODOVICK C. LEEDS. Enlisting at Oronoko, Michigan, Leeds joined the 25th Infantry. He was promoted to corporal and sergeant. In this image, he is holding an Enfield rifled musket. Leeds mustered out at Salisbury, North Carolina, in June 1865 and died in Dallas, Texas, on January 18, 1901. (Courtesy of Robert Coch.)

JAMES H. LYMAN AND HIRAM STEFFY. Both men enlisted in Company B, 3rd Michigan Cavalry, and were promoted through the ranks. Lyman (left) was commissioned a lieutenant on July 4, 1865, and Steffy was a sergeant. Lyman was from Shiawassee County and Steffy from Clinton County. Both men were mustered out on February 12, 1866, at San Antonio, Texas.

CHARLES W. MAYNARD. A resident of Ann Arbor, Maynard enlisted in Company D, 20th Michigan Infantry, as sergeant. At the Battle of Spotsylvania, he was wounded and taken prisoner. Maynard was commissioned lieutenant, Company C, in January 1865. In 1871, he graduated from the University of Michigan and established a pharmacy at 505 Second Avenue in Detroit.

EBENEZER W. MONROE. This tintype shows Monroe as a member of Company C, 3rd Michigan Cavalry. Born in Van Buren County, Monroe enlisted in the cavalry in September 1861. He was mustered out in October 1864 at Brownsville, Arkansas. In this image, Private Monroe is drawing a cavalry saber from its scabbard and has a Colt revolver tucked into his sword belt. His father was a cousin of Pres. James Monroe. A Republican, Monroe served as a highway commissioner and was a member of Benson Post No. 303 of the GAR.

JOHN W. ODELL. This carte de visite of Odell was taken by Baton Rouge photographer A.D. Lytle. Private Odell enlisted in Company B, 3rd Michigan Cavalry, in February 1864. He was placed on detached duty in November 1865, serving as an orderly for Gen. Philip Sheridan in New Orleans. (Courtesy of Richard Tanner.)

EDWIN B. PARKS (1838–1907). Living in Jackson, Michigan, Parks joined Company K, 1st US Sharpshooters. Corporal Parks shed his blood in four different battles. He survived wounds at Malvern Hill, Gettysburg, Petersburg, and Deep Bottom, and he was discharged at Petersburg in October 1864. Returning to Michigan, he married, fathered four children, and farmed near Stockbridge, where he is buried in Oaklawn Cemetery. (Courtesy of Dale Niesen.)

CHARLES PEEL. Born in England, Peel enrolled as an artificer in Company H, 1st Michigan Engineers and Mechanics. He fought in battles at Perryville, Kentucky, Lavergne, Tennessee, and Bentonville, North Carolina, and in numerous skirmishes. Peel was promoted to corporal and sergeant. Returning to Michigan when the war was over, he married and helped raise seven children in Oakfield Township in Kent County, where he had a farm. (Courtesy of Michael Hogle.)

JOHN PIERSON. In this photograph, Sergeant Pierson (right) poses with an unknown comrade. Pierson, from St. Clair County, enlisted in Company A, 7th Michigan Infantry, at Port Huron in August 1861. He was wounded in action at Cold Harbor, Virginia, in June 1864 and was promoted to first sergeant prior to mustering out of service in July 1865.

AUGUSTUS POMEROY AND COMRADES.
Two members of the 24th Michigan
Infantry are identified in this
image. Seated at right is 1st Sgt.
Augustus Pomeroy and standing at
left is Sgt. Charles Durfee. Pomeroy
was wounded at Gettysburg and
Dabney's Mill and was promoted
to lieutenant in March 1865.
Durfee, from Plymouth, was
discharged in December 1863 due
to wounds received at Gettysburg.

WILLIAM B. PRATT. A resident of Byron,
Pratt became a color sergeant with the
10th Michigan Infantry. He was promoted
to lieutenant and mustered out at
Louisville, Kentucky, on July 19, 1865.

CHARLES L. RICE. Enlisting at Detroit, Rice was a member of the 1st Company of Sharpshooters, which was attached to the 16th Michigan Infantry. He was promoted to first sergeant and commissioned lieutenant. Rice was discharged on a surgeon's certificate of disability in August 1863. In this image, he is holding a custom-built target rifle, which was extremely accurate when fired. (Courtesy of Dale Niesen.)

PRIVATES LEWIS L. AND JACOB B. SHARRATTS. This father and son enlisted as privates with Company K, 1st Michigan Engineers and Mechanics, at Grand Rapids in December 1863. Lewis died of disease at Ringgold, Georgia, during General Sherman's Atlanta Campaign. Lewis's father, Jacob, survived the war and was mustered out at Nashville, Tennessee. In this photograph, they are wearing kepis and frock coats and holding Enfield muskets and bayonets. (Courtesy of Dale Niesen.)

EUGENE KING STARKWEATHER (1842–1922). Residing in Plymouth when the war began, Starkweather enlisted as wagoner, Company D, 5th Michigan Cavalry, serving from August 1862 until June 1865 when he mustered out at Fort Leavenworth, Kansas. In this imposing tintype, Starkweather cradles his saber and has a pistol tucked into his belt. After the war, he lived and farmed in Plymouth Township and is buried at Oakwood Cemetery in Northville.

FRANK C. WHITE. This soldier from Grand Haven enlisted in the 14th Michigan Infantry as commissary sergeant in February 1862. White was commissioned lieutenant and quartermaster and discharged on March 14, 1865. He is buried in Grand Haven. (Courtesy of Robert Coch.)

Four

CAMP SCENES, FIELD MUSICIANS, AND UNKNOWNS

This chapter contains unique images of regimental bands, musicians, and drummer boys, as well as photographs of unknown soldiers. Daily camp routines included reveille in the morning, breakfast call, sick call, guard mount, drill call, dinner call, and battalion, regimental or brigade drill, dress parade, supper call, roll call, and taps. Dress parades were held in the evenings, even on Sundays. For parades, each company was formed by its orderly sergeant. The tallest men took the right of the company, the shortest men on the left. When the band struck up a march, each company was marched out in full dress by its company commander. After reviewing officers inspected the troops, the companies were marched back to their campgrounds and dismissed.

When in camp, the soldiers held dances, organized debating societies, enjoyed singing, and played fiddles, banjos, and harmonicas. Regimental bands often serenaded the officers. Often the men sang patriotic songs such as "The Star Spangled Banner," "Rally 'Round the Flag," "Maryland, My Maryland," and "John Brown's Body." The men enjoyed smoking pipes, writing letters, and playing cards, chess, or checkers. Mail call was a high point of the day, and the delivery of newspapers was welcomed.

The regimental commissary provided sufficient food and drink for the men, and the regimental quartermaster provided clothing, blankets, and tents. Every regiment had a sutler who sold all types of merchandise, including soap, candles, canned fruits, playing cards, socks, cups, identification badges, and many other items. When leaving camp and on the march, haversacks were filled with hardtack, salt pork, sugar, and coffee.

Regimental and brigade bands served important functions in camps. They practiced daily and provided musical entertainment for the soldiers, which enlivened the dull routines of camp life. Musicians participated in drills, parades, funerals, and even played music during battles. Their musical performances included marches, polkas, quicksteps, operatic airs, and patriotic songs. Bandsmen were cross-trained as stretcher bearers, first-aid providers, surgeons' assistants, and grave diggers. The final four images in this chapter are representative of the hundreds of unidentified soldiers' photographs that were examined for this publication.

4TH MICHIGAN SOLDIERS. This regiment, recruited from counties located in southern Michigan, fought in the Peninsula Campaign, the Seven Days, the Second Battle of Bull Run, Antietam, Fredericksburg, Chancellorsville, Gettysburg, and Grant's Overland Campaign. Achieving a distinguished record, it suffered high casualty rates. This carte de visite image shows three well-equipped soldiers with Austrian .54-caliber muskets, revolvers, and a Bowie knife.

PICKET GUARD ON ALERT. These unidentified members of the 4th Michigan Infantry are armed with Model 1855 US Rifled Muskets. Several soldiers wear distinctive hats and gaiters, which often appear in images of the 4th Michigan. (Courtesy of George Wilkinson.)

NONCOMMISSIONED OFFICERS. 3rd Michigan Infantry sergeants pose next to stacked .54-caliber Austrian muskets. Kneeling on the left is Sgt. Wallace W. Dickenson, Company K, from Newaygo. Later in the war, Dickenson was a lieutenant with the 10th Michigan Cavalry. This photograph was taken by Fred Heath from Grand Rapids, who made a series of 3rd Michigan images in the winter of 1861–1862. (Courtesy of Dale Niesen.)

FORT WOODBURY. Seven soldiers from the 4th Michigan Infantry strike a pose with a cannon at Fort Woodbury. Constructed in August 1861, this earthen fort located in Arlington, Virginia, was part of the defensive fortifications designed to protect Washington, DC. (Courtesy of George Wilkinson.)

TENT NO. 1, CAMP MICHIGAN. Pictured here in 1862 from left to right are John Shaw, Chandler Andrews, Ben Gardner, Herman Kusig, and James Jones, members of Company K, 3rd Michigan Infantry. Shaw was missing in action after the Second Battle of Bull Bun and discharged in January 1863. Andrews died of disease at Fort Monroe on June 19, 1862. Gardner was honorably discharged in June 1864. Kusig was wounded at the Second Battle of Bull Run and served in the Veteran Reserve Corps. Jones was discharged for disability in November 1862. (Courtesy of David Broene.)

10TH MICHIGAN CAVALRY. This image taken in the fall of 1865 shows officers and men of Company C, 10th Michigan Cavalry, posing for a final photograph. Gathered around two cannon, with their swallow-tailed guidon blowing in the wind, these troopers would muster out of service on November 11, 1865, and return to their civilian pursuits. (Courtesy of Dale Niesen.)

1ST MICHIGAN ENGINEERS. These officers relaxing in front of their tent are, from left to right, regimental surgeon William H. De Camp, Maj. Joseph J. Rhodes, and Lt. Col. Kinsman A. Huntoon. De Camp and Huntoon were honorably discharged in October 1864. Rhodes remained with the unit until it was mustered out of service in 1865. This photograph was taken near Bridgeport, Alabama. (Courtesy of John Gelderloos.)

5TH MICHIGAN CAVALRY. Officers gather in front of their winter quarters at Stevensburg, Virginia. This band of brothers includes, from left to right, Maj. Crawley Dake, Capt. Benjamin Axtell, Capt. Horace Dodge, Lt. Charles H. Stafford, Lt. Robert C. Wallace, and Lt. Walter Stevenson. Axtell was mortally wounded, Dodge discharged due to wounds, and Stevenson was accidentally killed when his horse fell on him in Detroit. (Courtesy of John Beckendorf.)

1ST MICHIGAN ENGINEERS. Standing in the right foreground is Capt. John W. McCrath, commander of Company B, 1st Michigan Engineers and Mechanics. The company stands in parade formation at its camp in Chattanooga, Tennessee. The officers and noncommissioned officers are positioned in front of the privates. This photograph was taken following the Battle of Lookout Mountain. (Courtesy of John Gelderloos.)

STAFF OFFICERS 22ND MICHIGAN INFANTRY. Col. Heber Le Favour (front left) poses with his staff for this photograph. Le Favour was captain, 5th Michigan Infantry, and seriously wounded at Williamsburg, Virginia, on May 5, 1862. Assigned to the 22nd Infantry in August 1862, he was commissioned regimental colonel in January 1863. Taken prisoner at Chickamauga, Tennessee, Le Favour was mustered out of service in June 1865. (Courtesy of the USAHEC.)

GATHERING OF NCOs. A balding Sgt. Alonzo Howard Merrick, Company C, 11th Michigan Infantry, sits on the right in this albumen photograph. Merrick was from Sturgis, Michigan, and was killed at the Battle of Missionary Ridge on November 25, 1863. He is buried in the National Cemetery at Chattanooga, Tennessee.

MOSES HOUGHTON AND STAFF. Seated on the porch of a Texas hacienda are, from left to right, Capt. George H. Rathbun, Company D, 4th Michigan; unidentified; Brigadier General Houghton, 3rd Michigan Infantry; Capt. Charles Fox, Company H, 4th Michigan Infantry; and unidentified. This carte de visite image was taken in Texas, where these regiments were stationed from July 1865 to May 1866.

13TH MICHIGAN INFANTRY BAND. The regimental band's 16 musicians posed for this photograph at Lookout Mountain in September 1864. The instruments include over-the-shoulder E-flat cornets, B-flat cornets, E-flat alto horns, B-flat basses, drums, and cymbals. (Courtesy of David Broene.)

4TH MICHIGAN INFANTRY BAND. In this photograph, the bandsmen carry over-the-shoulder saxhorns. This image was taken near San Antonio, Texas, on the Salado Rio. Pictured from left to right are Riley W. Cravens, principal musician Luther A. Haynes, Samuel B. Corbus, Isaiah Phair, Addison Hawley, Edmund Dodge, Frank Ingalls, Joseph Dodge, Eldridge S. Post, John Post, Hiram Ellis, Marvin Smith, William T. Fiester, Chancey J. Pickett, and Charles C. Hastings. (Courtesy of Pat DeHaan.)

WILLIAM T. MILLS. A resident of Kalamazoo, Mills enlisted in the 2nd Michigan Infantry Band, serving only three weeks prior to being discharged for disability. In August 1862, he joined the US Army as a musician, serving until August 1865. In this image, Mills holds an over-the-shoulder tenor saxhorn in B-flat. (Courtesy of David Broene.)

JAMES D. ELDERKIN. Holding an over-the-shoulder soprano saxhorn E-flat cornet, Elderkin stands at attention. In this carte de visite image, Elderkin, who served with the 1st and 5th Michigan Infantry Regiments, is wearing a Detroit Light Guard belt buckle. He served as a fife and drum major in the Army and was author of *Biographical Sketches and Anecdotes of a Soldier of Three Wars, as Written by Himself,* published in Detroit in 1899. (Courtesy of William Munday.)

JONATHAN WILSON. In August 1862, Wilson enlisted in Company G, 1st Michigan Engineers and Mechanics, in Kalamazoo. Performing with the regimental band, Wilson played the over-the-shoulder bass saxhorn in E-flat. Note the engineer's insignia on his kepi. (Courtesy of Robert Coch.)

JOHN PITTWOOD. Born in 1843 in England, Pittwood joined the 4th Michigan Infantry. At the First Battle of Bull Run, his thumb was shot off, and he was discharged. Later, Pittwood enlisted in the 1st Michigan Engineers and Mechanics as chief bugler and musician. Although he played an over-the-shoulder E-flat alto, in this photograph he holds a soprano saxhorn E-flat cornet with three-string rotary valves. He is also wearing an engineer's device on his kepi. After the war, he lived in Newago. (Courtesy of Robert Coch.)

IRON BRIGADE BAND. This carte de visite shows 16 members of the band with their over-the-shoulder brass saxhorns arranged around stacked drums. These musicians also received training in first-aid techniques and how to transport and care for wounded soldiers.

Drummer Robert Hendershot. Originally a member of Company C, 9th Michigan Infantry, Hendershot joined the 8th Michigan Infantry and became famous at the Battle of Fredericksburg. He attached himself to the 7th Michigan Infantry when it made an amphibious assault across the Rappahannock River and became known as the "Drummer Boy of the Rappahannock." Horace Greeley presented him a silver drum, and President Lincoln endorsed him for West Point. After the war, he toured the country playing his drum with his son Cleveland, who played fife.

Drummer Thomas Rhodes (1846–1925). Born in England, Rhodes enlisted as a drummer with Company G, 9th Michigan Infantry, at age 16. He reenlisted in August 1864, hoping to serve in the line, but Capt. Mortimer Mansfield, commander of Company G, took away his rifle and handed him a drum. Rhodes drummed for years in the Coldwater Light Guard and was known throughout the state as one of Michigan's top drummers. Rhodes is buried at Oak Grove Cemetery in Coldwater.

DRUMMER MARCUS F. JONES. This 14-year-old boy from Ionia County enlisted in September 1861 with Company E, 1st Michigan Engineers and Mechanics. Jones served with the regiment until May 1863. In this image, Jones holds drumsticks, while a black leather sling secures his infantry snare drum to his hip and leg. (Courtesy of John Gelderloos.)

DRUMMER WILLIAM H. WELSH. This Wayne County boy was mustered into Company A, 16th Michigan Infantry, in September 1861. He reenlisted as a musician in December 1863 at Rappahannock Station, Virginia, and was mustered out at Jeffersonville, Indiana, in July 1865.

DRUMMER WILLY YOUNG. Enlisting at age 13 in Company G at Detroit, he was the youngest member of the 24th Michigan Infantry. Young served from August 1862 to June 1865. This sixth-plate tintype was used as an illustration in O.B. Curtis's *History of the Twenty-Fourth Michigan of the Iron Brigade.* Young was a member of Detroit's GAR Post No. 384.

DRUMMER JOHNNY CLEM (1851–1937). In May 1863, Clem enlisted as a musician, Company C, 22nd Michigan Infantry. After the Battle of Chickamauga, he was promoted to sergeant and remains the youngest person promoted as a noncommissioned Army officer. In this image, he is posing with his hand on his hip, wearing sergeant's stripes and new boots. Clem made a career of the Army, retiring as a major general in 1915. He is buried at Arlington National Cemetery. (Courtesy of the LOC.)

UNKNOWN 7TH MICHIGAN INFANTRY. This is a carte de visite of an unknown private from Company A, 7th Michigan Infantry. His Hardee hat with decorative plume, the letter A, and infantry insignia are clearly visible. A revolver and knife are tucked into his waist belt, and shoulder scales are visible on his frock coat.

UNKNOWN PRIVATE. This tintype shows a private in the 24th Michigan Infantry of the Iron Brigade. The unidentified soldier stands at attention with his musket and is wearing his cartridge and cap boxes. (Courtesy of GNMP.)

UNKNOWN FIRST SERGEANT. This carte de visite is of a first sergeant, 5th Michigan Cavalry. His kepi has the brass crossed sabers, brass regimental number five, and letter designating Company K. The back mark is Benson, Photographer, Pontiac, Michigan. (Michael Hogle.)

UNKNOWN PRIVATE, 1ST MICHIGAN ENGINEERS AND MECHANICS. The private in this tintype is well armed with a musket, Bowie knife, pistol, bayonet, cap box, and cartridge box. The brass device on his hat is an engineer's castle.

Five

THE ULTIMATE SACRIFICE

Almost 15,000 Michigan soldiers died during the four years of the Civil War. Without a doubt, Michiganders contemplated their initiation into combat with a mixture of excitement, nervousness, and fear. None of these men anticipated dying, yet they often met a bloody and violent death on the battlefield. Many perished from wounds and diseases in hospitals and prison camps. For every Michigan soldier who died on the field of battle, two died from disease. The greatest causes of war deaths were diseases such as typhoid, typhus, and dysentery. Measles, pneumonia, diarrhea, and infections also took their toll. Soldiers who died in Confederate prison camps tended to be malnourished and vulnerable to disease due to unsanitary conditions, lack of clean water, and inadequate clothing and shelter.

Men realized that in battle, death could be a reality, whether it be instantaneous or a result of painful and long-suffering wounds that shattered their bodies. Many soldiers died following amputations or other surgical procedures that caused shock and erysipelas or gangrene infections, which rapidly spread through their bodies.

This chapter presents images of Michigan soldiers who gave their lives to preserve the Union. Col. Thornton Brodhead, 1st Michigan Cavalry, was mortally wounded at the Second Battle of Bull Run. In Brodhead's final letter to his wife, he wrote, "I fought manfully and now die fearlessly." Capt. Allen Zacharias, Company K, 7th Michigan Infantry, was killed at Antietam. Clutched in his hand was an envelope on which he had written, "I am wounded mortally, I think. The fight rages around me. I have done my duty . . . I left not the line until nearly all had fallen and colors gone. I am getting weak; my arms are free, but below my chest all is numb. The enemy [is] trotting over me, the numbness up to my heart. Good-bye, all. Your son, Allen." Capt. Wendell Wiltsie, Company G, 20th Michigan Infantry, was paralyzed when a bullet entered near his spine. He died two days later, requesting that his sword be given to his son, and with it he could fight for his country, were it ever assailed by traitors.

ALBERT BLUNT. Just before Christmas 1863, Blunt, a 43-year-old resident of Jefferson, Michigan, enlisted in Company K, 27th Michigan infantry. Five months later, on May 6, 1864, at the Battle of the Wilderness, Private Blunt was killed. (Courtesy of Robert Coch.)

MELVIN BREWER. He was commissioned captain, Company I, 1st Michigan Cavalry, in August 1861 at Almont and made a major in February 1862. Brewer was wounded at the Battle of Trevilian Station. Promoted to lieutenant colonel, he was mortally wounded at Winchester, Virginia, on September 19, 1864, dying several days later.

THORNTON F. BRODHEAD (1820–1862).
He was educated at Harvard, a Detroit
lawyer, journalist, postmaster, state senator,
and veteran of the Mexican-American
War. Colonel Brodhead organized the 1st
Michigan Cavalry and led them into battle
at Second Battle of Bull Run, where he was
mortally wounded. He was posthumously
brevetted brigadier general for gallant and
meritorious services. Brodhead is buried
in the family plot at Detroit's Elmwood
Cemetery. (Courtesy of the LOC.)

SIREL CHILSON. At the outbreak of the
war, Chilson lived in Van Buren County.
In August 1862, he enlisted in Company
D, 24th Michigan Infantry. Promoted to
corporal, Chilson became clerk for the
brigade quartermaster. He was commissioned
a lieutenant and adjutant in September
1863. At Petersburg, Virginia, Chilson
was detailed as an aide on Gen. Lysander
Cutler's staff. He was killed on June 18,
1864, only two weeks after receiving the
assignment. The fatal ball severed the
jugular vein and came out near his eye.

SAMUEL DE GOLYER. He served in the 4th Michigan infantry as a captain, Company F, and was captured at the First Battle of Bull Run. He managed to escape from the Confederates and was treated by the Northern press as a hero, the first Union officer to escape from the clutches of the rebels. He met Gen. Winfield Scott and Pres. Abraham Lincoln following his return to Federal lines. Commissioned a major, De Golyer accepted command of Battery H, 1st Michigan Light Artillery, which was assigned to the Army of the Tennessee. Mortally wounded at Vicksburg, Mississippi, he died on August 8, 1863. (Courtesy of George Wilkinson.)

JOHN GILLULY. A graduate of the University of Michigan's law school, Gilluly established his office in Brighton and was elected to the Michigan Legislature in 1859–1860. He was captain of Company I, 5th Michigan Infantry, and led his men through the Peninsula and Seven Days Campaigns. In August 1862, Gilluly was commissioned lieutenant colonel. At the Battle of Fredericksburg, he was killed while leading a successful counterattack to save the cannon of the 6th Rhode Island Artillery Battery. He is buried in St. Paul's Episcopal Cemetery in Brighton. (Courtesy of the Howell Area Archives.)

JOHN EGLER (1819–1864). This remarkably artistic sixth-plate tintype shows Private Egler with an apple in one hand, his identified backpack and blanket roll on the table, and a bayonet in the other hand. An old soldier of 43 when he enlisted in Company A, 26th Michigan Infantry at Centreville, Egler was mortally wounded at the Battle of Spotsylvania, Virginia, dying several weeks later. He is buried at Fredericksburg National Cemetery.

WILLIAM B. HUTCHINSON. A Detroiter, Hutchinson joined the 24th Michigan Infantry as sergeant in July 1862. He was commissioned lieutenant with Company C in April 1864 and was killed at the Battle of the Wilderness in Virginia on May 6, 1864.

WILLIAM E. LIMBARKER. His residence was in Lenawee County in 1861. Limbarker enlisted in Company F, 4th Michigan Infantry, as sergeant for three years. He was wounded on June 27, 1862, and captured at Gettysburg on July 2, 1863. Taken to Belle Isle Prison Camp in Richmond, Limbarker was killed by a Confederate prison guard while performing cleanup duty. He is buried in the National Cemetery in Richmond, Virginia. (Courtesy of George Wilkinson.)

JAMES B. MASON. At age 19, Mason, from Battle Creek, was commissioned captain in the "Merrill Horse" (a Missouri regiment) in June 1861. As the lieutenant colonel of the 11th Michigan Cavalry, he was killed leading a charge at the Battle of Saltville, Virginia, on October 4, 1864, in which his regiment suffered 86 troopers killed, wounded, and missing. (Courtesy of Richard Tanner.)

WALTER McCOLLUM. An 1861 graduate of the University of Michigan, McCollum studied a classical course and was a member of Delta Kappa Epsilon fraternity. At the time of enlistment, he was a member of the law department at the university. McCollum became captain, Company H, 20th Michigan Infantry, and was killed on May 12, 1864, during the Battle of Spotsylvania.

OFFICERS, COMPANY H, 20TH MICHIGAN INFANTRY. Pictured here from left to right are Horace Knight, Wendell Wiltsie, and Walter McCollum, graduates of the University of Michigan. Captain Knight was captured at Horse Shoe Bend, Kentucky, in May 1863 and not released until March 1865. His health broken, he died in 1867 and is buried at Forest Hills Cemetery in Ann Arbor. Captain Wiltsie, a law school graduate, recruited Company H, whose officers were made up entirely of university men. Captain Wiltsie was mortally wounded at Knoxville, Tennessee, and Captain McCollum was killed leading Company H at the Battle of Spotsylvania on May 12, 1864.

WILLIAM NOBLE. He was living in Detroit at the time of his enlistment as first sergeant with Company G, 2nd Michigan Infantry, in May 1861. Promoted to lieutenant in March 1862, Noble was appointed adjutant in December 1862. He served as aide-de-camp and provost marshal on the staff of division commander Maj. Gen. Philip Kearney in the Peninsular and Second Battle of Bull Run Campaigns until the death of General Kearney at Chantilly, Virginia, on September 2, 1862. Lieutenant Noble was killed in action at Knoxville, Tennessee, on November 24, 1863. (Courtesy of Dale Niesen.)

DAVID OLIPHANT. A Detroit resident, Oliphant was a lieutenant, Company B, 5th Michigan Cavalry, and commissioned a captain in December 1862. He was wounded in fighting at Brandy Station, Virginia, in October 1863. Captain Oliphant received a mortal wound fighting at Hawes's Shop, Virginia, on May 28, 1864, and died June 4, 1864. His friend, Lt. Col. Robert C. Wallace, wrote that Oliphant was one of the best officers in the regiment. (Courtesy of John Beckendorf.)

ANDREW G. PAISLEY. He lived in Speaker, Michigan, when he enlisted in Company K, 22nd Michigan Infantry, as sergeant in August 1862. Sergeant Paisley was taken prisoner at the Battle of Chickamauga, Georgia, on September 20, 1863, and died at Andersonville Prison Camp on June 20, 1864. Sergeant Paisley is buried in the National Cemetery in Andersonville, Georgia. (Courtesy of Dale Niesen.)

ISRAEL B. RICHARDSON (1815–1862). One of Michigan's most distinguished soldiers, Richardson graduated from West Point in 1841 and served in the Seminole and Mexican-American Wars. In 1855, he resigned from the Army and became a gentleman farmer in Pontiac. Following the bombardment and surrender of Fort Sumter, Richardson returned as a colonel with the 2nd Michigan Infantry. He fought at Bull Run and was promoted to brigadier general in August 1861 and major general in July 1862. At the Battle of Antietam, Richardson was mortally wounded by a ball from a spherical case shot. The general died on November 3, 1862, and his remains were taken to Pontiac's Oak Hill Cemetery. (Courtesy of the LOC.)

HORACE S. ROBERTS (1828–1862). The grand master of Michigan Masons was killed at the Second Battle of Bull Run, and his remains were never recovered. A cenotaph erected by Masons marks his grave at Detroit's Elmwood Cemetery. Colonel Roberts was a veteran of the Mexican-American War, former Detroit city clerk, register of deeds for Wayne County, successful merchant, and member of the Detroit Light Guard. As colonel, 1st Michigan Infantry, Roberts led them through the battles of the Seven Days, and at the Second Battle of Bull Run he was shot in the chest, living about 10 minutes. Prior to the battle, he told the regimental chaplain, "I trust that Michigan will believe that I tried to do my duty." (Courtesy of Michael Hogle.)

A. MORELL ROSE. At the outbreak of the war, Captain Rose was principal of Union Academy in Monroe. At the Battle of Malvern Hill, Virginia, on July 1, 1862, he fell while leading Company A, 4th Michigan Infantry. In 1880, Rose's valor and gallantry were recognized by veterans who named the Chippewa Lake GAR Post No. 389 in his honor. (Courtesy of George Wilkinson.)

WILLIAM J. SPEED. Detroit's city attorney, Speed was also a member of the Detroit Light Guard and possessed good knowledge of military tactics. He became captain, Company D, 24th Michigan Infantry. When the regiment was mustered in, members of the Detroit Bar presented him with a beautiful sword. At Gettysburg, on July 1, 1863, Speed was instantly killed when a bullet pierced his heart. (Courtesy of Robert Coch.)

EDGAR A. SPRAGUE. Enlisting at the age of 23, Sprague, who was from Marshall, was hospital steward for Company A, 8th Michigan Cavalry. During Gen. George Stoneman's raid on Macon, Georgia, Sprague was captured and listed as missing following the July 31, 1864, Battle at Sunshine Church in Jones County. Sprague was confined to prison in Macon, where he died on May 21, 1865. (Courtesy of Michael Hogle.)

JAMES H. TURRILL. Turrill, a married lumberman from Lapeer with two children, became captain of Company G, 7th Michigan Infantry. Captain Turrill was killed at Antietam, on September 17, 1862. The Lapeer GAR Post No. 144 was named in his honor. Turrill is buried at Mount Hope Cemetery in Lapeer. (Courtesy of Michael Hogle.)

FRANCES M. VANDERBURGH (1838–1863). Vanderburgh worked as a bank bookkeeper in Port Huron prior to the war. In November 1861, he joined Company E, 10th Michigan Infantry, as sergeant. Promoted to lieutenant, Vanderburgh was in charge of guarding a train on the Nashville and Chattanooga Railroad when, on April 10, 1863, it was attacked by guerrillas. In the ensuing fight near Antioch Station, Tennessee, Lieutenant Vanderburgh was shot three times and mortally wounded. He died on April 18, 1863, and his father returned his remains to Port Huron.

JOHN S. VREELAND. He enlisted in Company K, 1st Michigan Infantry, for three months. Then Vreeland became lieutenant and captain of Company A, 17th Michigan Infantry. While serving on the staff of Col. Benjamin C. Christ, commander of the 2nd Brigade, 3rd Division, IX Corps, Vreeland was killed in action at Spotsylvania, Virginia, on May 12, 1864.

MORRIS B. WELLS. A resident of Ionia, Wells joined Company B, 16th Michigan Infantry, as a lieutenant in July 1861. Transferring to the 21st Michigan Infantry as its adjutant in July 1862, he was wounded at Stones River, Tennessee. Commissioned lieutenant colonel in February 1863, Wells was killed at Chickamauga, Georgia, on September 20, 1863. He is buried in the National Cemetery at Chattanooga, Tennessee. (Courtesy of Robert Coch.)

THOMAS WILLIAMS. A Detroiter, Williams graduated from West Point in 1837. Assigned to the 4th US Artillery, he received two brevets in the Mexican-American War. Promoted to brigadier general in September 1861, Williams commanded a brigade in the operations to capture New Orleans. His brigade occupied Baton Rouge, where it was attacked on August 5, 1862, by the Confederate forces of John Breckinridge. During the fighting, Williams was shot in the chest by a rifle ball and killed. His remains were returned to Detroit, and he is buried in Elmwood Cemetery. (Courtesy of the USAHEC.)

DWIGHT A. WOODBURY. A successful Adrian hotelkeeper and colonel of a local militia unit, Woodbury was appointed colonel, 4th Michigan Infantry. At the Battle of Malvern Hill on July 1, 1862, he was instantly killed by a shot to the head. After the war, his remains were interred in Adrian's Oakwood Cemetery.

WILLIAM S. WOODRUFF. A resident of Calhoun County, Woodruff enlisted in Company F, 1st Michigan Infantry, in July 1861. In this carte de visite, he wears the rank of first sergeant. At the Second Battle of Bull Run, Woodruff was wounded and taken prisoner. He was commissioned lieutenant in December 1862, and at Gettysburg on July 2, 1863, Woodruff was wounded again. He commanded Company E on June 25, 1864, near Petersburg, Virginia, where he received a mortal wound. Woodruff died on June 28, 1864, at Armory Square Hospital.

GEORGE A. WOODRUFF (1840–1863). An 1861 graduate of West Point, he was assigned to Battery I, 1st US Artillery. During Pickett's Charge on July 3, 1863, while mounted on his horse, Woodruff was shot through the intestines, suffering immensely and dying at 4:00 p.m., July 4, 1863. His father, George Woodruff, a Calhoun County judge, traveled to Gettysburg and returned the lieutenant's remains to Marshall. He is buried in Oakridge Cemetery. (Courtesy of the USAHEC.)

Six

BRAVERY, GALLANTRY, VALOR, AND THE MEDAL OF HONOR

Soldiers who were recipients of the Medal of Honor received their awards in small, silk-lined wooden cases. Recognized for their bravery, gallantry, and valor, 52 Michigan men, representing the infantry, cavalry, sharpshooters, signal corps, and navy, were awarded the nation's most prestigious military medal. Acts of personal gallantry and courage by Michigan soldiers occurred on every bloody battlefield where they were engaged in combat. Infantrymen and cavalry troopers performed conspicuous acts of gallantry and distinction on dozens of battlefields. Lt. Thomas Custer, 6th Michigan Cavalry, was awarded two Medals of Honor for capturing flags of different Confederate regiments in the final weeks of the war. He is the only Civil War soldier that was twice presented this award. Other Michigan recipients included men of every rank from privates to generals. The citations explaining the actions for which the medal was awarded reveal soldiers who captured enemy flags, saved wounded comrades from prison or death, and used leadership abilities to rally men to attack or defend locations.

This chapter contains images of 13 Michigan Medal of Honor recipients, several of which have never previously been published. There were eight men in the 17th Michigan Infantry and eight in Company B, 47th Ohio (which was an all-Michigan unit), that received this medal. Lt. Frank Baldwin, 19th Michigan Infantry, received a second Medal of Honor in the Indian Wars. The selfless valor that sets these men apart from their comrades occurred at such well-known battlefields as Bull Run, Antietam, Peach Tree Creek, Spotsylvania, and Cold Harbor, as well as little-known actions like Newby's Crossroads, Grapevine Bridge, Lenior, Namozine Church, and Camden.

FRANK DWIGHT BALDWIN (1842–1923).
A resident of Constantine, Baldwin joined Company D, 19th Michigan Infantry, as lieutenant. This image of Baldwin was taken on October 5, 1863. He received two Medals of Honor: one for bravery at the Battle of Peach Tree Creek and a second in the Indian Wars. Baldwin died at Fitzsimons General Hospital in Denver and is buried at Arlington National Cemetery. (Courtesy of Dale Niesen.)

CHARLES BARRELL (1842–1914). He entered service in Allegan County as a private, Company D, 17th Michigan Infantry. Commissioned a lieutenant, Company C, 102nd US Colored Troops (1st Michigan Colored Infantry), Barrell received the Medal of Honor for rendering hazardous service near Camden, South Carolina, in April 1865. After the war, he worked as a salesman and banker. Barrell is buried at Hooker Cemetery in Leighton Township, near Wayland, Michigan.

THOMAS WARD CUSTER (1845–1876). General Custer's younger brother Tom enlisted in Company H, 21st Ohio Infantry. In July 1864, he was commissioned lieutenant, Company B, 6th Michigan Cavalry. This carte de visite, taken in Washington, DC, on January 3, 1865, at Mathew Brady's studio, shows Tom standing with his famous brother and sister-in-law Elizabeth B. Custer. Tom received two Medals of Honor for capturing Confederate battle flags at Namozine Church and Sailor's Creek, Virginia. He served in the postwar Army and was killed on June 25, 1876, at the Little Big Horn. (Courtesy of the LOC.)

CHARLES H. DEPUY (1842–1935). In August 1863, DePuy enlisted in Company H, 1st Michigan Sharpshooters. A sergeant at the Battle of the Crater on July 30, 1864, DePuy continued to fire abandoned cannon at Confederates until he was captured. He was a recipient of the Medal of Honor for his gallantry at the Crater. After the war, DePuy lived in Kalkaska and worked as a bookkeeper and carpenter. He is buried in Kalkaska's Evergreen Cemetery.

CORNELIUS MINOR HADLEY (1838–1902). In this carte de visite, Hadley poses with his wife, Minerva. He received a Medal of Honor for his service with the 9th Michigan Cavalry during the Knoxville Campaign. Hadley carried dispatches from General Grant to General Burnside through Confederate lines and brought back replies. After the war, he was a farmer near Litchfield, Michigan, where he is buried at Mt. Hope Cemetery. (Courtesy of Dale Niesen.)

EDWARD HILL (1834–1900). A Detroit resident, Hill entered service in Company D, Lancers, as lieutenant in October 1861. Appointed lieutenant with Company K, 16th Michigan Infantry, Hill was wounded at the Second Battle of Bull Run. Promoted to captain, he was wounded again at Cold Harbor, Virginia, on June 1, 1864. For his actions at Cold Harbor, he was awarded the Medal of Honor. Hill is buried at Fredericksburg National Military Cemetery, Virginia. (Courtesy of David Broene.)

SMITH HUGH HASTINGS (1843–1905). This tintype depicts Hastings, 5th Michigan Cavalry, in his field dress. On July 24, 1863, at Newby's Crossroads, Virginia, he helped repel a Confederate attack, saving two artillery pieces. He received the Medal of Honor for this action. Hastings was wounded at Trevilian Station, and in December he was promoted regimental colonel. After the war, he lived in Denver, Colorado, and is buried there in Riverside Cemetery. (Courtesy of the Archives of Michigan.)

BENJAMIN MORSE (1844–1908). Morse sits on the right in this tintype. Enlisting as a private with Company C, 3rd Michigan Infantry, Morse was captured at White Oak Swamp and wounded and captured at Chancellorsville, Virginia. At the Battle of Spotsylvania on May 12, 1864, Morse captured the flag of the 4th Georgia Artillery Battery, for which he received the Medal of Honor. He served as commander of the Joseph Wilson GAR Post No. 87 for 22 years and is buried at Oakwood Cemetery in Lowell. (Courtesy of Richard Tanner.)

WILLIAM RUFUS SHAFTER (1835–1906). In this postwar photograph, Shafter wears the Medal of Honor. Born in Galesburg, he was a lieutenant with Company I, 7th Michigan Infantry, at Fair Oaks on May 31, 1862. Although wounded, Shafter continued fighting until the close of the engagement. He received the Medal of Honor for this action. Shafter was major, 19th Michigan Infantry, colonel, 17th US Colored Infantry, and brevetted brigadier general for gallant and meritorious services. During the Spanish-American War, Shafter who was nicknamed "Pecos Bill," commanded the 5th Army Corps during the invasion of Cuba. Retiring in 1901 as a major general, he died in 1906 and is buried in the San Francisco National Cemetery. (Courtesy of Richard Tanner.)

FREDERICK WILLIAM SWIFT (1831–1916). As a captain with Company F, 17th Michigan Infantry, Swift's leadership abilities were quickly recognized, and he was commissioned lieutenant colonel. On November 16, 1863, at Lenoir, Tennessee, after three of his color bearers were wounded, he grabbed the regimental colors and had his soldiers form on him. Attacking Confederates were driven back, and the Union lines held. For his actions at Lenoir, Swift received the Medal of Honor. He is buried in Detroit's Elmwood Cemetery. (Courtesy of the USAHEC.)

ORLANDO BOLIVAR WILLCOX (1823–1907). Willcox served in the Mexican-American, Seminole, and Civil Wars. Appointed colonel, 1st Michigan Infantry, he was wounded and captured at the First Battle of Bull Run. Commissioned brigadier general in August 1862, he is recognized as one of the most prominent division commanders in the Union army. Willcox was awarded the Medal of Honor for gallantry at Bull Run on July 21, 1861. He was buried at Arlington National Cemetery following his death from acute bronchitis.

WILLIAM H. WITHINGTON (1835–1903). As a captain with Company B, 1st Michigan Infantry, Withington was wounded and taken prisoner at the First Battle of Bull Run. When released from captivity, he was appointed colonel, 17th Michigan Infantry. For his gallantry at South Mountain, Maryland, Withington was brevetted brigadier general. He received the Medal of Honor for aiding his wounded commander at the First Battle of Bull Run. He manufactured farm implements and served in the state legislature after the war. Withington is buried at Mt. Evergreen Cemetery in Jackson, Michigan. (Courtesy of Dale Niesen.)

ALONZO WOODRUFF (1839–1917). A member of Company I, 1st Michigan Sharpshooters, at the Battle of Hatcher's Run on October 27, 1864, Woodruff saved a wounded comrade. Pictured here is an aging Woodruff wearing a dark suit, with clear eyes, graying hair, and moustache with his Medal of Honor pinned to his lapel. There is a monument to Woodruff on the grounds of the Ionia County Courthouse. He is buried in Luther's Valley Cemetery. (Courtesy of the Luther Area Museum.)

Seven

VETERANS' MEMORIES AND MONUMENTS

In the spring and summer of 1865, Confederate armies surrendered, the Union was restored, slavery abolished, and the need for large federal armies ceased to exist. Soldiers mustered out of service and returned to their homes and civilian occupations. Veterans' organizations were created, including the Grand Army of the Republic (GAR) and the Military Order of the Loyal Legion of the United States (MOLLUS). Any Union veteran was invited to become a member of the GAR. Union officers and their male descendants could obtain a membership in MOLLUS.

Friendships fostered in military camps were renewed and strengthened in these veterans' organizations. Annual encampments and reunions were held at local, state, and national events, where veterans gathered, shared, and relived memories of service. Souvenirs distributed at these events included ribbons, badges, jewelry, official guides, programs of activities, magazines, books, and clothing items. Two national GAR encampments were hosted in Detroit and three in Grand Rapids. On May 30, 1868, Memorial Day was established by the GAR as a day to decorate the graves of comrades who died in defense of their country.

GAR posts were often named to honor and memorialize soldiers who died in battle. Monuments were erected in communities and placed on courthouse grounds or cemeteries. Detroit commissioned a beautiful monument to honor its soldiers and sailors. Algonac erected a bronze statue of a soldier on a granite base located in Boardwalk Park. Grand Rapids commissioned a zinc fountain depicting a soldier at parade rest, which was restored and rededicated in 2003. In Lansing, on the lawn of the state capitol, are monuments to Gov. Austin Blair, the 1st Michigan Sharpshooters, and the 1st Michigan Engineers and Mechanics. The Michigan State Legislature funded monuments that were placed at battlefields, including Gettysburg, Vicksburg, Chickamauga-Chattanooga, and the Andersonville Prison site. The GAR and MOLLUS were politically influential and lobbied for veterans' benefits and pensions. The legacies and traditions of Civil War veterans are continued by their descendants in organizations such as MOLLUS, the Sons of Union Veterans of the Civil War (SUVCW), the Women's National Auxiliary to the Sons of Union Veterans of the Civil War, and the Women's Relief Corps (WRC).

RICHARD AVERY AND SON. With their drumbeats, the Averys entertained GAR posts with their musical abilities. Richard Avery served in Company A, 9th Michigan Infantry, and was mustered out at Nashville, Tennessee, in September 1865. Avery was a member of Detroit's Francis U. Farquhar GAR Post No. 162. In this cabinet card photograph, Avery and his son proudly wear ribbons identifying the Farquhar post.

RALPH ELY POST GAR. This unidentified member of the Ralph Ely GAR Post No. 127 in Shepherd, Michigan, proudly holds the post flag. He stands at the entrance to a tent with a female relative. This GAR post and the WRC raised necessary funds to erect a soldier's monument at Coe Township Cemetery. (Courtesy of Robert Coch.)

THEODORE HOENNINGHAUSEN. A member of Company E, 16th Michigan Infantry, Hoenninghausen was famous for playing one of the bugles signaling the surrender at Appomattox Court House. In this formal portrait, he is holding his bugle. After the war, Hoenninghausen was a retail merchant in Detroit who sold tea and coffee. (Courtesy of John Gelderloos.)

JOHN A. PATTEE (1844–1924). A resident of Huron, Pattee (second from left) joined the 24th Michigan and served throughout the war. An accomplished fiddler since childhood, in postwar years he organized a group called Old Soldiers Fiddlers. In this photograph, the message of reconciliation is obvious. Pattee attended Michigan Day at Gettysburg and was a member of the GAR's Fairbanks Post in Detroit. (Courtesy of Dale Niesen.)

ANDERSON MINER. A resident of Bushnell, Miner enlisted in Company D, 9th Michigan Infantry, in September 1861. He was discharged in October 1862 for disabilities. After the war, Miner lived in Petoskey. In this photograph, he wears a post commander's badge and medal from a Chicago veterans' event. (Courtesy of the Luther Area Museum.)

WILLIAM A. CHILDS. In 1862, Childs was living in Copper Harbor when he joined Company B, 27th Michigan Infantry. Promoted from sergeant to captain, Childs was noted for his valor at the storming of Fort Mahone on April 2, 1865. After the war, he lived in Calumet and was active in veterans' affairs. In this image, he wears a MOLLUS medal and Michigan State Seal uniform buttons. (Courtesy of Glen Fincham.)

FRANK M. HOWE AND VELOROUS W. BRUCE. Howe (left), from Emmett, joined Company C, 20th Michigan. Wounded at Petersburg, his left leg was amputated. Bruce, from Adrian, joined Company A, 17th Michigan. Wounded at Campbell's Station, Tennessee, Bruce's right leg was amputated. In this image, the two comrades pose arm in arm. "United We Stand, Divided We Fall" is written on the photograph. (Courtesy of Glen Fincham.)

JAMES F. MCGINLEY GAR POST NO. 201. Members of Manistee GAR Post No. 201 pose for this photograph taken in 1908. In the image are seven veterans from Michigan, six from Wisconsin, five from Ohio, four from New York, two from Pennsylvania, and one each from Indiana and Illinois, plus a navy veteran. The silk GAR post banner in the background is displayed at the Manistee Museum. (Courtesy of the Manistee Museum.)

7TH MICHIGAN INFANTRY REUNION. Capt. James McPherson hosted a reunion of veterans at his home in Lowell on June 13, 1893; McPherson holds his grandchild on his lap. Seated in the center with his drum is Johnny Spillane, wearing a gold medal recognizing him as the "Drummer Boy of the Rappahannock."

22ND MICHIGAN INFANTRY REUNION. On August 19, 1917, surviving members of the 22nd Michigan Infantry pose for their 50th reunion photograph on the steps of Pontiac's old city hall. Their tattered regimental and national colors are proudly displayed. One veteran holds the iconic cowbell that was rung when the regiment marched into battle. Daughters of Union Veterans of the Civil War sponsored the event and provided dinner for the old soldiers.

1ST MICHIGAN CAVALRY REUNION. These old veteran troopers, Company D, 1st Michigan Cavalry, gathered to share war stories and memories on August 20, 1886. They all wear reunion ribbons, have boutonnieres in their lapels, and several have GAR brass insignias on their hats. The location of the reunion is unknown.

5TH MICHIGAN CAVALRY. Posing for a reunion photograph are 16 veterans who served in Company A, 5th Michigan Cavalry. Lt. Samuel Harris (middle row, far right) is the only identified person in the image. Harris lived in Chicago after the war and published numerous booklets about the 5th Cavalry, as well as his *Personal Reminiscences*. (Courtesy of John Beckendorf.)

BEAR LAKE REUNION. The second annual reunion of the Bear Lake Association of Soldiers and Sailors was held September 6–9, 1910. A village of tents was organized at Lakeside Park, including a large commissary tent where food was provided for the veterans. A drum corps and cornet band provided martial music, and during the day cannon salutes were fired. (Courtesy of the Manistee Museum.)

FRANKFORT REUNION. GAR members held reunions and marked special anniversaries with encampments. On Memorial Day, lilacs were laid on the graves of those veterans who had passed, speeches were given, and dramatizations performed. In the summer of 1889, Frankfort hosted a GAR encampment and erected tents for the veterans along First Street. Note the wooden-planked sidewalks, veterans in the street, musicians, drums, and flags. (Courtesy of the Benzonia Museum.)

10TH MICHIGAN CAVALRY. A reunion of veteran troopers from the 10th Michigan Cavalry was held in 1897. Pictured here in attendance are, from left to right, (first row) Libious P. Graves, Daniel Flanigan, John Runyan, James McLaughlin, and Edward Skinner; (second row) David B. Averill, Gilbert M. Randall, Charles P. Wilson, Charles H. Anderson, and John W. Ellison. They all wear reunion ribbons, and several have GAR membership badges on their coats. (Courtesy of Dick and Mary Hutchins.)

WADELL GAR POST No. 120. Old soldiers proudly holding the flag climbed aboard this wagon in September 1898 for Howell's Floral Parade. Their GAR post was named for Lt. Andrew D. Waddell, who recruited local men to serve in Company I, 5th Michigan Infantry. Many of these veterans decorated the graves of their comrades on Memorial Day. (Courtesy of the Howell Area Archives.)

GETTYSBURG MICHIGAN DAY. This steel engraving was used to illustrate formal programs and souvenir ribbons distributed to veterans and their families attending the June 12, 1889, dedication of Michigan's Civil War monuments at Gettysburg. Hundreds of Michigan residents made the pilgrimage to Pennsylvania to participate in ceremonies dedicating monuments to the 1st, 3rd, 4th, 5th, 7th, 16th, and 24th Infantry Regiments, as well as Michigan Sharpshooters, Michigan Cavalry Brigade (1st, 5th, 6th, and 7th Regiments), and 9th Michigan, Battery I, 1st Artillery.

Cavalry Brigade Monument. An eight-foot-tall cavalry trooper stands atop a 40-foot-high granite monument dedicated to Michigan's Cavalry Brigade. Many veterans attended the dedication, including, from left to right (starting from the far left), former governor Austin Blair, Gen. James Kidd, Gen. Russell Alger, and Gen. Luther Trowbridge. On the monument, located on the Rummel farm, are bronze plaques representing the 1st, 5th, 6th, and 7th Cavalry Regiments and a bas-relief medallion of General Custer. (Courtesy of Roger Heiple.)

5TH MICHIGAN MONUMENT. Veterans of the regiment gathered at Gettysburg for the dedication ceremony conducted by Gen. John Pulford. The granite monument, depicting a soldier in the act of loading a musket, is located just west of the Wheatfield, where the 5th Michigan Infantry placed its regimental colors during the battle. (Courtesy of Roger Heiple.)

24TH MICHIGAN MONUMENT. Known as the Wayne County Regiment, 126 veterans with regimental and brigade flags marched from Gettysburg to the location of their monument. Maj. Edwin B. Wright gave the dedication address, and the song "Sweet Bye-and-Bye" was sung in memory of fallen comrades. A life-sized figure of a soldier loading a musket stands on top of the granite pedestal. (Courtesy of Roger Heiple.)

SOLDIERS' AND SAILORS' MONUMENT. This monument was dedicated on Detroit's Woodward Avenue on April 9, 1872. Attending the unveiling were Gen. George Custer, Gen. Philip Sheridan, Gen. Ambrose Burnside, and 25,000 spectators. The bronze and granite sculpture contains statues representing branches of the military, medallions of Lincoln, Grant, Sherman, and Farragut, and an Indian queen representing Michigan. The inscription honors Michigan's heroes who fought in defense of liberty and union. (Courtesy of the LOC.)

HOWELL'S CIVIL WAR MONUMENT. The dedication of Howell's monument took place on Memorial Day, May 30, 1895. The soldier atop the monument stands at rest and looms vigilant at the entrance to Lakeview Cemetery. GAR members, Sons of Union Veterans of the Civil War, and WRC ladies marched behind Howell's Cornet Band for the patriotic ceremony. Hazen Pingree, Detroit's mayor and Michigan's future governor, was the keynote speaker.

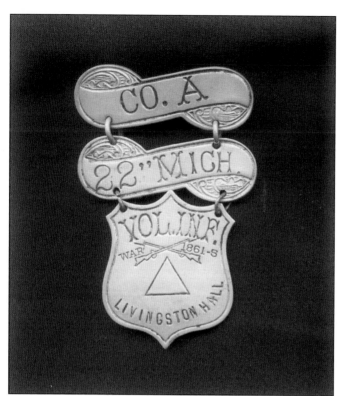

LIVINGSTON HALL'S VETERAN'S BADGE. At age 19, Hall enlisted as a musician in the 22nd Michigan Infantry at Farmington. His postwar residence was in Reed City. As this photograph reveals, his name is engraved on the silver veteran's badge and identifies Hall as a member of Company A, 22nd Michigan Volunteer Infantry. (Courtesy of Robert Coch.)

7TH MICHIGAN RIBBON. Veterans of the 7th Michigan Infantry wore ribbons like this at the GAR's 25th National Encampment held in Detroit in August 1891. The trefoil, or three-leaf clover, was the symbol of the II Corps, Army of the Potomac, to which the 7th Michigan Infantry was assigned. Today, Civil War veterans' ribbons are highly prized and collectable.

BIBLIOGRAPHY

American Biographical History of Eminent and Self-Made Men of the State of Michigan. Vols. I & II. Cincinnati: Western Biographical Publishing Company, 1878.

Bak, Richard. *A Distant Thunder: Michigan in the Civil War.* Ann Arbor: Huron River Press, 2004.

Beyer, Walter F., and Oscar F. Keydel, eds. *Deeds of Valor.* Vols. I & II, Detroit: The Perrien-Keydel Company, 1906.

Cullum, George W. *Biographical Register of the Officers and Graduates of the US Military Academy at West Point, New York.* Vols. I & II. New York: D. Van Nostrand, 1868.

Heitman, Francis B. *Historical Register and Dictionary of the United States Army.* Vols. I & II. Urbana, IL: University of Illinois Press, 1972.

Hunt, Roger D. *Brevet Brigadier Generals in Blue.* Gaithersburg, MD: Olde Soldier Books, Inc. 1990.

————. *Colonels in Blue: Michigan, Ohio, and West Virginia.* Jefferson, NC: McFarland and Company, 2011.

Lanman, Charles. *The Red Book of Michigan: A Civil, Military and Biographical History.* Detroit: E.B. Smith and Company, 1871.

Record of Service of Michigan Volunteers in the Civil War. 46 Volumes. Kalamazoo: Ihling Brothers and Everard, 1905.

Robertson, John, compiler. *Michigan in the War.* Revised edition. Lansing, MI: W.S. George, 1882.

Warner, Ezra J. *Generals in Blue.* Baton Rouge: Louisiana State Press, 1972.

Welsh, Jack D., M.D. *Medical Histories of Union Generals.* Kent, OH: The Kent State University Press, 1996.

DISCOVER THOUSANDS OF LOCAL HISTORY BOOKS FEATURING MILLIONS OF VINTAGE IMAGES

Arcadia Publishing, the leading local history publisher in the United States, is committed to making history accessible and meaningful through publishing books that celebrate and preserve the heritage of America's people and places.

Find more books like this at
www.arcadiapublishing.com

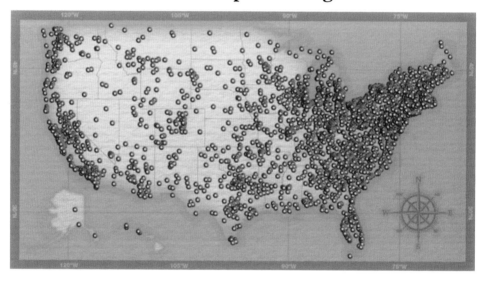

Search for your hometown history, your old stomping grounds, and even your favorite sports team.